DOCUMENTING LOCALITIES

A Practical Model for American Archivists and Manuscript Curators

RICHARD J. COX

The Society of American Archivists
and
The Scarecrow Press, Inc.
Lanham, Md., & London

SCARECROW PRESS, INC.

Published in the United States of America
by Scarecrow Press, Inc.
4720 Boston Way
Lanham, Maryland 20706

4 Pleydell Gardens, Folkestone
Kent CT20 2DN, England

British Cataloguing-in-Publication Information Available

Library of Congress Cataloging-in-Publication Data

Cox, Richard J.
    Documenting localities : a practical model for American archivists
and manuscript curators / Richard J. Cox.
        p.   cm.
    Includes bibliographical references and index.
    ISBN 0-8108-3043-4 (alk. paper)
    1. Archives—United States. 2. United States—History, Local—
Archival resources. I. Title.
    CD3021.C69   1996
    025.2'814'0973—dc20   96-28802

ISBN 0-8108-3043-4 (cloth : alk.paper)

⊖™ The paper used in this publication meets the minimum requirements of
American National Standard for Information Sciences—Permanence of
Paper for Printed Library Materials, ANSI Z39.48-1984.
Manufactured in the United States of America.

CONTENTS

PREFACE

Christopher Lasch, in the most important revisionist interpretation of the concept of progress, *The True and Only Heaven: Progress and Its Critics* (1991), made a statement that suggests one of the many challenges modern archivists face in the late twentieth century:

> Our collective understanding of the past has faltered at the very moment when our technical ability to recreate the past has reached an unprecedented level of development. Photographs and motion pictures and recordings, new techniques of historical research, the computer's total recall assault us with more information about history— and everything else—than we can assimilate. But this useless documentation no longer has any power to illuminate the present age or even to provide a standard of comparison. The only feeling these mummified images of the past evoke is that the things they refer to must have been interesting or useful once but that we no longer understand the source of their forgotten appeal (p. 112).

Somehow the archivist must deal with all this documentation to ensure that the records with continuing value to their creators and society will be identified, preserved, and made available for use. This task is not easy. Its difficulty is evident in the continuing debate in the archival literature about the nature and purpose of the archival appraisal function, a debate that has not reached any real broad consensus but has produced some interesting theoretical and methodological concepts (such as the archival documentation strategy).

This volume is part of a series of volumes concerning the nature of American archival theory and practice. Whether these works eventually constitute a systematic statement of archival science as practiced in the United States remains to be seen, but it is clearly my intention to prepare some additional volumes expounding on important and interesting themes and issues introduced or suggested in earlier publications. As such, *Documenting Localities* is closely connected to two earlier works.

In my *American Archival Analysis: The Recent Development of the Archival Profession in the United States,* I tried to sketch the significant events and trends, some still ongoing, that characterized the archival community in this nation in the 1970s and 1980s. In that volume I repeatedly referred to the importance of archival appraisal and its more recent uses, techniques, methodologies, and theoretical expositions. Archival documentation strategies, the main topic of the present book, were described in several places and were the subject of a full chapter, suggesting their significance to new work in this archival function. In that volume I tried to convey the notion that archival documentation strategy was not intended as a substitute for other archival appraisal approaches but was a model mechanism striving to resolve some standard problems in archival appraisal. I also tried to make clear that the archival documentation strategy required both additional testing and continued refinement. While offering some very practical advice for conducting such macroappraisal (as such approaches are now generally termed) as represented by the archival documentation strategy, I have reiterated the theme for continuing testing and refinement in this volume. In this latter sense, I affirm my belief that while we have guiding principles, methods and practices will continue to change and new ones will be introduced as needed.

While *American Archival Analysis* was my effort to sum up recent activity in the American archival profession, my more recent book, *Managing Institutional Archives: Foundational Principles and Practices* (New York: Greenwood Press, 1992), was an attempt to deal with a particularly notable absence of efforts in the encouraging, establishing, and nurturing of institutional archives in the United States. Outside of government archives the American archival profession has focused on collecting manuscripts and archival records, in many cases leaving behind a lacuna which the archival documentation strategy was partly intended to correct. That volume was written primarily as an introductory text for those individuals and organizations involved with, or interested in, the sustenance of institutional archives. It was written in the conviction that the age of collecting or acquiring, which has largely dominated the activity of American archivists, was over, even though the archival community had pursued such activity for many decades.

It is important to stress where archivists are in the preservation of our documentary heritage. Individual collecting was important before 1900 because archival and historical manuscript repositories were only then developing and were insufficient to preserve all valuable documentary materials. By the middle of this present century (in fact, probably long before then), the need for individual collectors had diminished because of the array of repositories. However, given the immense proliferation of records in the present information age, it is obvious that collecting programs must become repositories of last resort and the archival profession must move to encourage the creation of institutional archives. The technological possibilities of providing comprehensive metadata about archival holdings for researchers and even the electronic dissemination of full texts to remote sites lessens the disadvantages associated with the increased decentralization of archival records. Archival documentation strategies, as described in this book, can aid archivists and allied professionals with such work.

This present volume on documenting localities is intended to be a companion to *Managing Institutional Archives*. I have written this present book with a strong belief that the acquisition of archives and manuscripts must be far more systematic than it has been and, furthermore, that such acquiring of manuscripts and archives will always be unsuccessful if attempted without a commitment to establishing institutional archives. In this work I have tried to discuss the importance of the locality to American archival practice, the primary methods archivists have used to acquire documentation about localities, the practical basis of the archival documentation strategy as a more systematic approach to archival appraisal, and, finally, to suggest a schema for conducting such documentation work. A brief concluding chapter discusses additional sources of information on archival appraisal and the documentation strategy concept.

I offer this volume as a contribution to archival *practice*. Some will disagree with this, because they will note that it is built about a model or mechanism. In the ongoing battle about theory and practice, some are quick to view anything not completely emanating from nuts-and-bolts practice as being theoretical in nature. This view is extremely unfortunate. As Frederick Stielow has nicely stated it, in his "Archival Theory Redux and Redeemed: Definition and Context Toward a General Theory," *American Archives* 54 (Winter 1991), theory is "simply the codification of rational and systematic thinking, the conscious development of general principles or guides to explain or analyze" (p. 17). That is precisely what I have intended in this volume. Just as explicit perspectives, models, and theories can aid students grappling with complex historical issues, I am convinced that a conceptual model for documenting localities can aid archivists and manuscript curators wrestling with a task as complex and as confusing as the documenting of a specific geographic region.

One more prefatory note is in order. There has been increasing discussion about the role of the archivist in appraisal and, more broadly considered, in their institutions and society. While American archivists have stressed the notion of informational value, others have focused on evidence. Unresolvable conflict seems apparent. My perspective is different, and it underpins this book. First, I concur that the focus should be on evidence—the records-capturing transactions of continuing value because of legal, administrative, and fiscal needs. However, there is so much evidence that needs to be maintained and this evidence is so rich and deep that the informational needs of researchers and society will be more than met. Second, starting from the perspective of informational value—the wide-ranging interests, desires, and needs of a very diverse group of scholars and others— either overwhelms the archivist or, just as important, leads this professional to be tempted to preserve anything and everything. Third, the documentation strategy model is a mechanism that can aid archivists to get more precisely and quickly to the essential evidence. This strategy assists archivists in defining and limiting documentary objectives, identifying institutional archives that should be established or

strengthened, and resisting preserving documentary frag-
ments because of faulty or vague informational values.

ACKNOWLEDGMENTS

The sources for this book will be obvious to those who follow the continuing debate about archival appraisal. I first heard about the archival documentation strategy at a Society of American Archivists session in 1984 featuring Helen Samuels, Larry Hackman, and Patricia Arronson and immediately used it (albeit crudely) in some work I did for the District of Columbia Historical Records Advisory Board about the nature of cooperation between district archival and historical manuscripts programs. In 1985, while a Fellow at the Bentley Historical Library at the University of Michigan, I had the opportunity to discuss the concept with Larry Hackman and Joan Warnow-Blewett, who, as Fellows, were collaborating on their seminal *American Archivist* essay on this topic. The next year I joined the staff of the New York State Archives with a responsibility to test the documentation strategy on a regional level (a test discussed in this volume, adapted from an earlier *American Archivist* essay) and, in this regional test, I collaborated again with Hackman and others, such as Samuels and Timothy Ericson, who were continuing their experimentation with the idea. During the years 1987-1991 I worked with Helen Samuels and Timothy Ericson in developing and offering a series of workshops on the archival documentation strategy. It was in this effort that I refined my final ideas on the documentation strategy, moving far away from the limited procedural ideas held by individuals such as Larry Hackman.

This book owes its origins to these workshops and a series of papers that I presented at conferences from 1988 to 1991. The first chapter was originally sketched out in my mind for a half-day presentation at the Society of Mississippi Archivists meeting in 1989. The second chapter was influenced

by my background preparation for a workshop at the Association of Canadian Archivists meeting in 1991. Chapter
three has developed from two presentations, one at the 1988
American Association for State and Local History and the
other at a 1990 Urban History Conference at the Chicago
Historical Society. Chapter four was originally drafted in
1988 as a supplement to a self-study manual for historical
records programs published by the New York State Archives.
Due to philosophical and other differences, this supplement
was never published, and I offer this chapter as one means
of conducting local documentation analysis.

As the above comments suggest, I owe a variety of serious
debts to a number of individuals. Terry Cook and James M.
O'Toole offered many instructive comments on a draft of this
manuscript; I even followed some of their advice. Luciana
Duranti, Timothy Ericson, and Helen Samuels have been
continued sources of advice and criticism about archival
appraisal and documentation. Individuals such as David
Bearman and Avra Michelson have been steady sources of
advice about archival matters. Even reading and participating in the electronic Archives Listserve has helped me to
reflect on my own ideas and approaches, although much of
what is in this volume will not please some of the regular
combatants on the Listserve.

Richard J. Cox

1

The Importance of the Locality in American History and American Archives

THE LOCALITY'S PERSISTENT SIGNIFICANCE

The geographically defined locality, in concept and in reality, has had a major influence on what American historians and archivists have been doing throughout the twentieth century, even farther back if one accepts the notion that these disciplines were founded in this country in the nineteenth century. This chapter is an effort to describe what this influence has been on these two related disciplines, although the primary focus of this chapter and the book is the archival profession. This chapter is also an attempt to demonstrate that the locality will continue to exert a significant influence on these professions' activities, theories, and methodologies, despite the homogenizing influences of late twentieth century society that seem to threaten the wiping away of the individual's and society's sense of locality. Yet, as will be seen, the importance and value of the locality seems to persist.

What are some of these modern homogenizing influences in late twentieth century America? And what have they meant for our sense of the locality? It has been suggested that computers and their supporting networks, one of the most typical of modern society's features, "will touch our lives" in many ways, including redefining the concept of locality. "The neighborhoods we play in and the people with whom we do business no longer need be the ones close by but the ones we choose."[1] Individuals will work at home, communicate with colleagues around the world from their home and office, and gain access to electronic databases from personal computers sitting on their desks in the home, office, and even hotel rooms that were at one time only available at the largest of research libraries. Distinctions once associated with an individual's place, or that person's sense of place, may disappear. Philosopher Michael Heim has captured the nature of the tension here, writing that "digital writing turns the private solitude of reflective reading and writing into a public network where the personal symbolic framework needed for original authorship is threatened by linkage with the total textuality of human expressions."[2] Today, many individuals, sitting in front of their computers, are, by that simple act, connected to a large-scale information network that can transform not only their work but their perception of self and place.

What are some of the other types of homogenizing influences in modern American society? Advertising, transformed into its modern form and influence because of the capability of information and communications technologies, also brings the outside world into the local community in order to get that community to fit into purchasing trends and demographic predictions. Don Gifford noted that

> the average urban dweller in the United States is exposed to five thousand advertisements per day; few of us, even in small towns, could qualify as other than urban....Once, in 1940, I stood on a busy street corner in Boston and read all the signs and slogans I could see to a blind friend. We were there—and astonished—for over half an hour. But that seems simplicity itself when I compare it to the flood of sound and image on radio and TV and in the newspapers and in the supermarkets and malls and boutiques and in the clutter of catalogs—nine pounds per week—in our mail box.[3]

Confirmation of such homogenization is easy to come by; travel to different cities often brings an individual to shopping malls or districts virtually indistinguishable from ones in other places. Disorientation can be a fairly common problem under such circumstances. Alvin Toffler, in his popular analysis of societal change twenty years ago, noted that "place...is no longer a primary source of diversity. Differences between people no longer correlate closely with geographical background....Many people no longer stay in one place long enough to acquire distinctive regional or local characteristics."[4]

Some attribute to television a similar leveling impact, as does Bill McKibben. McKibben writes that

> I don't fret about TV because it's decadent or shortens your attention span or leads to murder. It worries me because it alters perception. TV, and the culture it anchors, masks and drowns out the subtle and vital information contact which the real world once provided.[5]

As one result, McKibben suggests, the "local and regional matter less and less and the national and global more and more."[6] These kinds of conclusions seem to be compatible with Marshall McLuhan's assessment that the "full-blown city coincides with the development of writing — especially of phonetic writing, the specialist form of writing that makes a division between sight and sound."[7] Again, it is easy to think about the influence of the personal computer and electronic writing and reading on all of this. So we can begin to understand something of the close relationship between local community and modern communication, information, and records. And, furthermore, such commentary has been made for at least a century, from the time of James Bryce's *The American Commonwealth,* a volume published in 1888 that at least partly considered the impact of mass communication on modern society.[8]

But in all these changes, despite concerns by people like Toffler and others, individuals still associate strongly with their geographic locality. After all, commentators have been discussing the declining impact of the locality on Americans for the past several centuries. We do have numerous factors tearing apart the locality and its importance to the individual and to society, while at the same time other factors buttress the locality (see Figure 1-1). Dr. Alexander Hamilton reflected in 1744, at the conclusion of this colonial excursion, that he "found but little difference in the manners and character of the people in the different provinces."[9] In the late nineteenth century, as another example, citizens groups and business-men rallied to fight the growing popularity of the large department store chains because they "threatened the American way of local life."[10] Other commentators have noted that whether there is a real local community or not, Americans have persisted in their quest for this locality or fabricated a mythology of such local community,[11] a phe-nomenon that perhaps owes something to the fact that the American concept of community is as much a religious or philosophical notion as it is a product of place.[12] Bill McKib-ben's worries, described in his *The Age of Missing Informa-tion*, are still reduced by the fact that the "earth...is local, small, particular. Television tells us we have everything in common. But we don't. And as we lose our particularity we lose prodigious amounts of information."[13] Still, writers like McKibben seem to have faith that aspects like the locality and its particular informational values will not only persist but prevail.

This notion of geographic place resists, in a variety of ways, the modern homogenizing influences of modern soci-ety. Don Gifford's penetrating contrasting analysis of the locality in the late eighteenth century with it two centuries later argued that the individual often consciously worked to reestablish a stronger sense of his or her immediacy and environment.[14] In the United States of the early nineteenth century, Robert Wiebe has shown how individual and com-munity were linked to other concepts of state and nation. Wiebe noted that "to express the natural affinity between individual and community, Americans attributed precisely the same characteristics to both." He concluded that "what linked the individual to the community then proceeded along a sequence of state to region to nation, and what charac-terized the smaller units applied in turn to each larger one: inherent values and linear destinies, times of trial and bursts

EXAMPLES

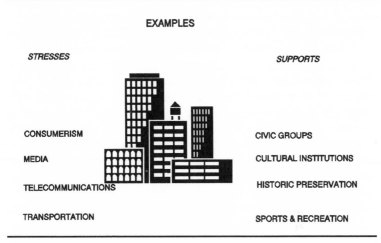

STRESSES

SUPPORTS

CONSUMERISM

CIVIC GROUPS

MEDIA

CULTURAL INSTITUTIONS

TELECOMMUNICATIONS

HISTORIC PRESERVATION

TRANSPORTATION

SPORTS & RECREATION

Figure 1-1. Examples of Stresses on, and Supports for, the Prominence of the Locality

of opportunity, the horrors of corruption and the wonders of conversation."[15]

We can see other examples of this. In the nineteenth-century city, according to Gunther Barth, "city people coined their cultural forms out of the new social and economic institutions forged in the modern city." Barth further commented that

> fortified by their cultural diversity, they devised answers to their most pressing urban problems. In the apartment house they adapted private space to a spatially divided city. They received from the metropolitan press the pieces of an urban identity and a language for communicating with each other. The department store assured women a place in city life, and they in turn made downtown the center of urban elegance. In the ball park men were exposed to the meaning of rules in the modern city and to that basic form of urban leisure, watching others do things. The vaudeville house brought a sense of common humanity to diverse people, who emerged from the experience with social skills and cultural values that helped them cope with the intricacies of metropolitan life.[16]

In all activities, it is possible to perceive individuals strug-
gling for new meanings in a rapidly changing society.

Similarly, as the technology of the nineteenth century
American industrial revolution took root, Americans adapted
it to build new communities, such as in Lowell, Massachusetts.[17] Even the American highway system has been characterized as a mechanism for catering to the American's
"sense of separateness," his or her search for identity, and
as "close as anything we have to a central national space," a
"national promenade."[18] Add to this the construction of
major information transmission systems from the eighteenth
century to mid-nineteenth century, characterized by many
as breaking down local barriers,[19] and we discover that they
did not diminish the importance and nature of the locality.
Finally, many contemporary planners have assumed a new
perspective towards the locality. As Tony Hiss states

> The land-use experts are convinced that three different forms
> of connectedness—the sense of kinship with all like; the sense
> of partnership with working landscapes; and the sense of
> community and companionability that is traditionally fos-
> tered by villagers and urban neighborhoods—can be main-
> tained in or, if necessary, brought back to even the most
> densely settled districts, old and new.[20]

The evidence of the significance of the locality is, therefore,
somewhat overwhelming in its magnitude. Sometimes its
persistence can be seen when a locality or a portion of it is
threatened in some manner. Kevin Lynch, examining the
nature of historic preservation, suggested this when her
noted that

> Many symbolic and historic locations in a city are rarely
> visited by its inhabitants, however, they may be sought out
> by tourists. But a threat to destroy these places will evoke a
> strong reaction, even from those who have never seen, and
> perhaps never will see, them. The survival of these unvisited,
> hearsay settings conveys a sense of security and continuity.[21]

Naturalists and ethnographers have chronicled similar
kinds of resistance to change in local settings which suggest

the importance of the locality to individuals, families, and communities.[22]

While the reasons for these links may have changed, Americans still seem to possess many identities ranging from immediate community to the nation and their nation's role in the world. these identities are consistently reevoked by defenders of local history. A half-century ago one professional historian suggested this when he wrote that

> The community is a world in miniature. Every thought the human mind ever entertained was conceived within a local setting. Every deed that was ever done was performed within the limits of some neighborhood. The world is the sum total of its communities. It inevitably follows that local community embraces everything that ever happened. Within a community it is conceived, written, read, and understood. The local historian writes the history of a church, a racial group, a fraternity, a school, or even a cemetery. In so doing he encompasses a more or less complete entity which in turn is related to larger entities.[23]

Fay Metcalf and Matthew Downey, in their more recent general guide to local history in the classroom, enumerate many of the other values associated with this variety of historical research and writing. They note that the "local neighborhood, town, or city, much like the family or the ethnic group to which one belongs, are social realities that help provide individuals with a sense of identity."[24] David Kyvig and Myron Marty, in their analysis of "nearby history," also contend that an understanding of local history is basic to individual self-awareness. "Indeed, your own past and that of people closest to you, family and community, have had a great impact on you. Learning about it enhances your memory and helps you comprehend influences on your life."[25] Bernard Norling, in his brief undergraduate textbook on historical study, expressed a similar sentiment and one typical of such textbook writers.

> Each city, county, or district cherishes its own past in the same way as an individual. If this past is to be preserved it has to be written down. The habit of keeping records and thereby storing up the accumulated knowledge and wisdom

of many generations is one of the obvious marks distinguish-
ing man from the rest of the animal kingdom. Consequently,
there are national, state, and local historical societies and
museums; written histories of virtually every state, city,
district, institution, church, and ethnic group; and of every
intellectual, political, economic, or social movement in the
land. One cannot drive far in any direction without encoun-
tering markers bearing the information that here is the oldest
Presbyterian church north of the Missouri river, there the site
of a battle in some Indian war, or there the place where West
Virginia's state constitution was written.[26]

Like any topic in the past of a nation, there are inherent
contradictions in the importance of the geographic locality
in its relationship to regional, national, and even international views and perspectives, much as Michael Kammen has
written about in his studies.[27] We have gone through periods
of particular emphases on one form of history versus another. The early nineteenth century was a time of great
interest in local historical research, writing, publication, and
preservation, hard on the heels of a period of time when
nationalism was stressed to create a distinct tradition and
self-respect for a new-found country. The rise of scientific
professional history at the turn of the century quickly transformed itself into a desire for grand theme national histories,
evident by the dramatic shift of the Johns Hopkins University history department, led by Herbert Baxter Adams, from
local studies to national and international studies. While
there has always remained a persistent interest in local
studies, it has shifted in and out of favor with fairly regular
clockwork. For local history archives and historical manuscript repositories, however, an important institutional type
for nearly two centuries, such changing patterns of interest
has only meant differences in the kinds of researchers using
their holdings.
    There may be many reasons why archivists and users of
archival records and historical manuscripts emphasize the
locality. This stress on locality may be a more convenient
defining attribute for collecting of sources or for documenting an area. It may be the result of historical development or
tradition in which local historical repositories were formed

as a means of providing community status and stability. Or, it may be because researchers have found the records conveniently stored and accessible and the topics for research more manageable than sweeping national views. These reasons, and others, will be explored in the remainder of this book.

A DEFINITION OF LOCALITY AND ITS HISTORY

Despite many attributes assigned to local history research and the often local orientation of this nation's manuscript and archival repositories, there are many problems and issues faced by such institutions that have not been adequately resolved by the archival profession. These problems and issues will be introduced in this chapter and will be addressed in subsequent chapters. Before going too far it is important, however, to define locality as used here. Carol Kammen, in her useful book on local history, stated that she saw "local history as the study of past events, or of people or groups, in a given geographic area — a study based on a wide variety of documentary evidence and placed in a comparative context that should be both regional and national."[28] I would like to build on Kammen's definition to suggest that a locality, in the context of this book, is that geographical area (from neighborhood to county or city to region) that an individual identifies with because of cultural, political, socioeconomic, historical or other reasons. David Russo has added to this that, as well, "students of community allow the people whom they study to say what a community is. The people who live in them have always had some perception of what communities are."[29] There are many elements that can be drawn upon for defining the nature of a specific locality (see Figure 1-2).

Archivists, residing and working in localities, will often develop practical suggestions for what a locality should and can be, just as historians themselves have done. Historian Darrett B. Rutman has noted that "community is real—the concurrence of group and place—but so diverse a social phenomenon as to defy every attempt to define it in terms of specific behavioral characteristics or values." Still, Rutman

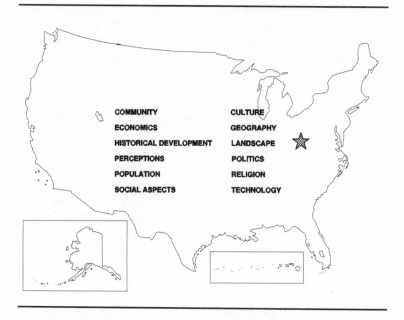

Figure 1-2. Some Defining Elements of a Locality

has noted the need to develop some pragmatic definition by establishing some working assumptions. By community, he wrote, "we conceive the subject to be simply the people of any particular locale, the pattern of their associations among themselves and with others beyond the locale, and, over time, the changes in that pattern." Rutman sees ordered associations among people, "related to landform, distance, and technology," and affected by "social topography," and "formed by networks."[30] On a more practical bent, the Chicago Neighborhood History Project has worked out a configuration of people, space, and time to develop a working definition of local community.[31] As will be seen in this and the other chapters, the precise definition of locality is that most rooted in the particular needs of the archivists and their colleagues. It may shift to suit the needs of the archival programs, historical manuscripts repositories, and the users of the holding of these institutions.

A useful example of what I am describing can be seen in a recent essay by historian John Mack Faragher, proposing what he terms a "relational" model or community. His definition provides an example of the kind of model which can be selected by researchers and archivists in guiding their work on the documentation or localities.

> A community is, first, an system of ecological relations. Historians must ask about community patterns of land and water use, distinctive modes of production, and the process of creating a local landscape as the setting for community life. Second, a community is a system of reproductive relations. There are important historical questions to ask concerning the age, gender, and ethnic composition of communities, their social stratification, the relations among what might be called community *members* (men, citizens, landlords) and community *subjects* (women, minorities, the landless or impoverished), as well as the struggles among these groups over the definition and control of public culture. Third, a community is a field for collective action. Historians of communities must discover the particular dialectic between collective and individual action, the alternating force of cooperation and competition in economic life, the centrifugal and centripetal forces of neighboring, the role of kinship, religion, and other local institutions in creating social networks. Finally, a community is a set of affective bonds. We need to know about the role of shared communal sentiment in cementing social relations, about the creation of local and regional identity, about the use of the community as a base of support for individuals and families.[32]

It is not difficult to see such a model for use in identifying and preserving documentation and as a means for analyzing records and manuscripts already held by archives and historical manuscripts repositories. The use of such models will be discussed later in this volume.

THE LOCALITY AND AMERICAN HISTORICAL RESEARCH

An appropriate place to begin a fuller analysis of the importance of the locality is with researchers' interest in local

historical research. Despite efforts by archivists and manuscript curators not to be the mere weathervanes of historiographical trends,[33] it is still the case that the origins,
development, and present nature of many of these archival
repositories were the products of the work of antiquarians,
local historians, and later, professional historians. It is also
the case that many of the existing archives and historical
manuscript repositories continue to be greatly affected by
the trends of historical research with a local orientation.
Historical researchers sit on the governing boards of such
programs. They continue to influence the definition and use
of institutional collection policies, and they assist in the
determination of what documents should be preserved in the
repositories.

The American professional (or academic) historian's interest in local history research has been, at best, cyclic in
pattern over the past century, falling in and out of favor for
a variety of reasons. Anniversaries, significant national
events and traumas, and other such occurrences, along with
the changing orientation to historical research and writing
have affected local history (see Figure 1-3 for a representation of this). In the late nineteenth century, some of the
first professional historians, such as Herbert Baxter Adams
and John Franklin Jameson, recognized the locality as a
laboratory to be studied. In the early 1920s Clarence H.
McClure, examining mainly what was going on in professional history, wrote that "local history is a field that is but
little worked in this country. As a people we care little for our
history. Family history is neglected. Few Americans can tell
anything about their great grandparents. Community history is seldom thought of and yet there are usually a few
people in every community who could easily be interested in
community history."[34] A generation later, others were noting
a shift in interest to local history because the historian was
"interested in social, economic, cultural, and intellectual
history" and "one of the best ways of pursuing such study of
the past is by doing it on the local level."[35] David J. Russo
has shown how the local historian dominated historical
writing throughout the nineteenth century and, in fact, for

1876 CENTENNIAL   1976/77 BICENTENNIAL/ROOTS

1880-1930 HISTORICAL PAGEANTS   1960-PRESENT NEW SOCIAL HISTORY

1880-1900 CIVIL WAR REGIMENTAL HISTORIES/MEMOIRS

1940 AASLH ESTABLISHED

1880-1920 SCIENTIFIC HISTORY

1900-1940 STATE ARCHIVES MOVEMENT

1870-1900 VANITY LOCAL HISTORY PRODUCTION

1820-1880 HISTORICAL SOCIETY MOVEMENT

| 1800 | 1850 | 1900 | 1950 | 2000 |

Figure 1-3. Selected Influences Stimulating Local Historical Research and Writing

the initial few decades of the twentieth century both academicians and antiquarians focused on the locality.[36]

The shifting patterns of interest in local history continued. Nearly forty years later, professional historians such as Roy P. Fairfield were reflecting their new-found interest in local history by trying to explain to their amateur colleagues that they must be aware of the more "professional" methods: "It is the function of the local historian in this moment of rapid flux to use modern historical methods creatively, to become so aware of national movements that his provinciality is objectified, to save records from the onslaught of 'progress,' and to capture his region's uniqueness while it is capturable."[37] In the early 1970s, Van Beck Hall tried to reassure local and amateur historians that new, seemingly nonhistorical, approaches to studying history were essentially a rediscovery of the locality.

Yet, this new emphasis on society, social theory, and statistics actually increases the number of persons and groups whose historical importance can and should be assessed. When historians asked questions dealing with great events or wrote biographies of famous men, the masses of people, communities, and families served only as a backdrop, while the spotlight fell on the event or the man. The shift toward social science merely means that many historians have now become more interested in looking at these previously unrecognized people and have found that all sorts of economic, social, cultural, religious, political, and many other differences existed among them. They also found that a great deal of important and exciting history can be written by describing these differences - how the people changed with time and the impact that the difference and the changes had upon the development of a community, region, state, or nation. In order to describe and analyze these differences, historians have borrowed some analytical tools from other disciplines, most of which can be used by skilled amateurs.[38]

Resting comfortably underneath this research activity has been the steady work of antiquarians, local historians, archivists, history museum curators, and others with deeply vested interests in documenting and interpreting the locality or, at the least, preserving some of its documentary remnants and artifacts. In any period of time it is possible to identify important local histories, but it is also true that there are greater clumps of quality studies on the locality in more recent decades than in earlier ones. Gilbert Fite, for example, has stated, as have many others, that "one of the most notable developments in the study and writing of American history during the last generation has been the rise to prominence of local, state, and regional history."[39] Kathleen Neils Conzen commenced her review of work completed on local history in the 1960s and 1970s by stating that "after almost a century in the historiographical wilderness, the history of life at the local level emerged in the 1970s as one of the most lively and promising areas of historical inquiry in the United States."[40]

Many reasons have been offered for the resurgence of interest by the academic historian over the past two or three decades. Conzen linked the interest in the locality to the historians' new-found concern in the 1960s in the inarticulate and history from the "bottom up." She noted that these historians gravitated to the locality because the sources were concentrated and "increasing numbers [of historians] began to realize that concentration on national history and emphasis on progress, shared experience, and democratic values had taken no account of major elements in the American past."[41] Robert Dykstra and William Silag have posited two reasons for this phenomenon. Cities, villages, and towns "have been deemed uniquely important, deserving singular scholarly treatment." These localities have also lent themselves to studies that "have generated results that add to our substantive, our theoretical, or our methodological knowledge in general" and that also manage "to say something about American culture in general."[42] Gilbert Fite said that the new interest in local history was that a "few professionals saw the rich opportunities in local and state history and began to exploit them."[43] Others have seen the study of local history as a panacea to society's problems. Russell Fridley, writing in the turbulent late 1960s, stated that "to a fragmenting society that seems increasingly devoid of meaning to an alarming number of its citizens, the study of local history can make at least four contributions: immediacy, identity, perspective, and an acceptance of change."[44]

But the most interesting and provocative reason for the interest in local history has probably been the significance of the locality to the individual's own self-identity, not dissimilar to the reasons why geneology and family history have grown in popularity in the same last quarter of a century.[45] Some Early American historians, such as Louis B. Wright, have argued that the pioneer settlers strove to make their new homes as much like their own native localities as was possible.[46] Other commentators on American life have extended this view to try to demonstrate that even in a mobile society such as the United States, a sense of the locality is important and, perhaps, even heightened.[47] This philosophy can be seen even in the popular histories churned out since the mid to late nineteenth century. Academic historians, such as Gilbert Fite, have been hypercritical of these local histories because they "consisted of glowing accounts of the leading pioneer families and superficial discussions of the community's institutions such as schools, churches, businesses, and lodges. The so-called histories could be best characterized as dull pubic relations efforts."[48] But these manifested weaknesses also reveal that the locality was a crucial part of an individual's and community's identity and purpose; otherwise, the "glowing" histories would not have been produced in the great numbers that they were and still continue to be, nor would there have been as many arguments as there have been through the years for the value and use of local histories and local history sources in all levels of classrooms.[49] To a large extent, these poorer relations in the local historical research represent efforts to make sense of the locality by its residents.[50] They are themselves documents (or artifacts) of the interest in the meaning of place for American citizens.

The value of even poor local history for an understanding of our post has been described by many historians. Bruce Catton suggested this when he commented on the influx of Civil War regimental histories that appeared in the generation after that conflict. On these histories, Catton mentioned that "most of them, considered strictly as histories, are very bad." Catton used such terms as "ineptly written" and even suggesting their deliberate falsification of history.[51] Yet Catton perceived great value in these histories.

> In the strictest sense of the world these were *local* histories. They were put together by men who just wanted to preserve the story of something that had happened to *them*, usually with no particular thought that they would ever have a wide usefulness. Essentially, they are part of the story of the town or the county or the region. No single one of them is of much value to anyone but the regionalist, the antiquarian, but in the end, all of them put together make up an essential part of the history of our country as a whole. The men who wrote those histories did a much greater service than they ever knew.[52]

Thomas Clark, looking at the panorama of the early local historian's work, has argued that "historians of every degree of disciplinary maturity" owe these writers because "[t]hey have preserved the personal stories of Americans who were founders and prime movers all across the land....Whatever they wrote, whether in flamboyant heroic style or in a sober and matter-of-fact one, they added a rich human dimension to the understanding of our national past."[53]

This service extends at least partly from the antiquarian foundation of the early local historians' work. Classicist Arnaldo Momigliano provided a clue to this in his definition of the antiquarian.

> Throughout my life I have been fascinated by a type of man so near to my profession, so transparently sincere in his vocation, so understanding in his enthusiasms, and yet so deeply mysterious in his ultimate aims: the type of man who is interested in historical facts without being interested in history. Nowadays the pure antiquarian is rarely met with. To find him one must go into the provinces of Italy or France and be prepared to listen to lengthy explanations by old men in uncomfortably cold, dark rooms. As soon as the antiquarian leaves his shabby palace which preserves something of the eighteenth century and enters modern life, he becomes the great collector, he is bound to specialize, and he may well end up as the founder of an institute of fine arts or of comparative anthropology.[54]

It was precisely this kind of individual who populated the American localities in the eighteenth and nineteenth centuries, and their activities (and collections) led to both the writing of many local chronicles and the formation of local historical repositories.

The so-called New Social historians have used the locality as a means of understanding the importance of common human activity and the people who carry out such activity. This use of the locality has prompted these historians to look at a greater wealth of documentation or evidence concentrated on smaller geographical settings or, as it is often referred to, to practice "microhistory." Jim Sharpe, describing such historical research, has noted that

> Two or three decades ago many historians would have denied the possibility, on evidential grounds, of writing serious history about a number of subjects which are now familiar ones: crime, popular culture, popular religion, the peasant family. From medievalists trying to reconstruct the life of peasant communities to oral historians recording and describing the life of earlier generations in the twentieth century, historians working from below have shown how the

imaginative use of source materials can illuminate many
areas of history that might otherwise have been though of a
doomed to remain in darkness.[55]

Collaboration on documentation and appraisal between archivists and researchers, such as these social historians,
should provide some illumination and aid the cause of
realistic and meaningful selection for preservation from the
vast quantities of information sources that are being created
daily. However, as David Russo has noted, this new kind of
social historical methodology has separated local and academic historians in ways that seem irreversible.[56]

These comments represent, of course, only the tip of the
iceberg in the past and present activity in local historical
research. Any visit to a local archives or historical manuscripts repository is likely to bring an encounter with a
tremendous diversity of researchers: an individual searching
for evidence about the construction date of a recently pur-
chased old house; another looking for the engineering records of an old bridge which needs renovation or
replacement; individuals searching for their family roots; a
lawyer accumulating information for a court case; a medical
researcher working on genetic or environmentally caused
diseases; a meteorologist considering the past weather patterns in the region; and a history professor studying the
patterns of ethnic communities in an urban setting. An
additional examination of the previously published volumes
on a locality will undoubtedly uncover a large number of
histories ranging from the work of antiquarians through civic
and community groups to that of historical scholars.

LOCAL HISTORY, HISTORIANS, AND ARCHIVISTS

There is, of course, a connection between what historians
are doing with local history and the local documentary
approaches of archivists. One aspect of this connection is
because of what sources for research are readily available
for consultation and study. Dykstra and Silag are rather
straightforward in their characterization of this symbiosis,
suggesting that "a number of highly respected local case

studies can be faulted less on grounds of atypicality [or other reasons] than by virtue of being based on source materials far less than perfect in quality."[57] Fite has noted that, in his opinion, "local and state history has flourished along side, and in conjunction with, the strengthening of local and state historical societies. The reason for this is obvious. These societies were and are the custodians of vast quantities of research materials that have formed the basis for many of the outstanding articles and books dealing with local and state history."[58] Indeed, at least some successes of quality historical research on localities are directly due to imaginative researchers who work with archivists in establishing significant archival programs documenting the locality.[59]

The precursors of the first repositories for historical manuscripts and archives were the early historians and collectors. Thomas Jefferson's interest in historical research and collecting has been well documented. In 1823 he wrote in a letter "that it is the duty of every good citizen to use all the opportunities which occur to him, for preserving documents relating to the history of our country," "our country" referring to Jefferson's state of Virginia.[60] As has also been well accounted, Jefferson's interest in this was because of his greater interest in "usefulness," "his definition of *usefulness* was an inclusive one, embracing the production of intellectual and aesthetic pleasure as well as of material comfort."[61] Jefferson's notions were pervasive in the Revolutionary and Early National eras, although much of his views were also directed to looking for principles and laws that guided the *national* history and development.[62] Peter Force, Jared Sparks, Jeremy Belknap, and a whole host of other collectors, editors, and historians seemed to follow such Jeffersonian concepts.

From the eighteenth through the nineteenth centuries, the establishment of repositories for historical manuscripts and archives were often the direct activities of local historians who needed places to maintain the sources they were using. Everything was up for acquisition. In the absence of government repositories, the private, quasipublic, and public historical societies scurried to gather the papers of individuals and families and the archives of organizations and

government agencies. The only driving motivation was the
records' potential use by a historical researcher. The formation in 1844 of the Historical Society of the University of
North Carolina reveals such a sentiment. At its first anniver-
sary and in its first report it determined to have a purpose
to preserve primarily Revolutionary War records: "Although
it cannot consider itself at all committed to the labor of
preparing such a stable record of Revolutionary events as is
understood by the term history, yet the simplest form of its
duty will be to render accessible to the historian, whoever he
may be, as far as possible, *all* the facts which may be
connected with the war in North Carolina."[63] Such notions
were commonplace. The movement for state historical societies and state archives were generally led by individuals
using the records and who desired their preservation and
more convenient use.[64] The many efforts for editing and
publishing historical sources were generated by such concerns as the preservation of useful materials for research,
compounded by a fairly wide public fascination with the
source materials. In the first half of the nineteenth century,
for example, there was such interest because of the "new-
ness" of the American past; in the words of George Callcott,
"every man *was* his own historian, searching for himself in
the old manuscripts and colonial records, enjoying the mys-
terious lore of the unknown, standing at the frontier of
knowledge."[65] The vast array of repositories populating the
American landscape suggest that the acquisitions of sources
for local history has never really abated since the founding
of the first state historical society in Massachusetts in 1791.

Yet, there is the general perception of the discovery and
rediscovery of the notion of local history. For many years at
least, national and local history *writing* co-existed peacefully.
If anything, it has been when the academic historians have
reflected on American historical research itself that they
have been most prone to castigate local histories or, with the
same result, move national history writing to the prominent
positions in the discipline's evolution and significance.[66] In
the nineteenth century, during the first stages of the founding and nurturing of historical manuscripts and archival
repositories, there was also intense interest in national and

universal historical writing, the study of the past on the grandest of all themes.[67] These interests have often, then, had different relationships at different periods, but it is important to realize that the work of institutions with a particularly well-focused local mission has steadily gone on. Much of our perception of the work on local history may be extremely prejudiced by the academic, scholarly historians who we have tended to read and believe. Critics of the historical profession, such as Theodore S. Hamerow, have shown that the in vogue scholarship has separated the historians from their former publics: "To our society, then, the methodology of historical scholarship appears inadequate for an understanding of the world in which we live."[68]

THE LOCALITY AND AMERICAN ARCHIVES: SYMBIOSIS AND THEORY

If local history writing and reading is part of an individual's effort to understand him or herself, then surely the collecting and preserving of local historical records, material culture, and architecture is also an important part of that effort. Earlier in this chapter it was mentioned that there was a natural relationship between the work of the local historian and the archivist, one providing grist for the other's mill, but the relationship being even more symbiotic than that. Local history sources are more popularly believed to be monuments to the past as well as sources. A senior editor of the Pittsburgh *Post-Gazette* once wrote about what he perceived to be the disappearing past of his region's industrial development; in his lament he noted "the curious fact that in Pittsburgh—so renowned in the industrial history of the world—there currently is no place to take a visitor to visualize that contribution." Part of the difficulty in this visualization was the loss of archival records, since "as steel mills were closed in the early 1980s, many records, photographs, and the like were discarded."[69] This newspaper man advocated support for the local historical society's efforts to raise funds and public support for a regional history facility that could display more artifacts and collect more source material.

Other such calls abound. Anthropologist-historian Anthony F. C. Wallace has also suggested the rationale for the careful preservation of a diversity of historical sources in even an intimate small community over a relatively brief period of time.

> Today...only a few members of the community recall much about these happenings....Time has flattened out, like the optical perspective of a landscape seen through a telephoto lens, and word-of-mouth transmission of unwritten historical information has slowed to a trickle. With each death of a participant, a whole world of information dies too; for the most part only written records and physical constructions remain. And these dwindle away constantly. Records are lost, paper crumbles, old letters are thrown away, unlabeled photographs become meaningless. And the mills, dams, races, tenements, bridges—all these too are subject to constant erosion....Each year less and less information is left of a world that was once as rich and real as the one that is there today.[70]

Such sentiments have long inspired individuals involved with the repositories of the past. Oft-quoted, for example, are Jeremy Belknap's 1790s calls for an extremely active Massachusetts Historical Society. First, he stated that "we intend to be an *active,* not a *passive,* literary body; not to lie waiting, like a bed of oysters, for the tide (of communication) to flow in upon us, but to *seek* and *find,* to *preserve* and *communicate* literary intelligence, especially in the historical way." Then, Belknap added at a later date: "There is nothing like having a *good repository,* and keeping a *good lookout,* not waiting at home for things to fall into the lap, but prowling about like a wolf for the prey."[71] Such sentiments were supported by strong convictions about the utility of the past in the activities of the present. As Henry D. Shapiro has suggested, individuals in the late eighteenth to mid-nineteenth century saw the

> collection of information...[as] a precondition to the development of an understanding of how the world worked in all its aspects. And because the world was presumed to work in one and only one way, information from the past could prove as useful as information from the present.[72]

COLLECTORS

REPOSITORY MISSIONS

AMATEUR HISTORIANS

PUBLIC INTEREST AND
AWARENESS

ARCHIVAL STANDARDS AND
METHODOLOGIES

HISTORICAL RESEARCHERS

CIVIC EVENTS

MEMORIALIZING THE PAST

Figure 1-4. Significant Influences on the Acquisition and Preservation of Local History Sources

The symbiotic relationship between local historian and archivist or manuscript curator—while complex in its many facets (see Figure 1-4)—can also be seen by understanding that the repositories of local historical records were born in the same culture as that that prompted more serious analysis of local history. T. J. Jackson Lears has carefully described the antimodernism of the period 1880-1920, the same period that saw the rise of professional history, the continued growth of historical societies, the establishment of new government archives, and the nascent beginnings of a modern American archival profession. Lears, in looking at the Boston Museum in this period, has captured some of what was occurring in many other cultural institutions, including archives and historical societies.

> One can see the social significance of the collections most clearly in the light of a more general enthusiasm for premodern emblems of authority. There was, for example, an unprecedented interest in genealogical pedigrees and coats-of-arms around the turn of the century. Genealogy merged class-consciousness with racism. As class and racial fears heightened, many Americans longed for the Nordic purity supposedly guaranteed by medieval antecedents. Genealogical societies multiplied: the Aryan Order of St. George

(1892) and the Baronial Order of Runnymede (1897) were two
of many formed during this period. The Lenox Library in New
York set aside a genealogical room in 1896. With the same
professional care displayed by artistic connoisseurs, genealogists justified claims to coat-armor. Intended only to satisfy
their wealthy clients, their work nevertheless had wider social
consequences. It provided an upper class under stress with
valuable emblems of unity and exclusiveness.[73]

The formation of archival and manuscript repositories also
served as such emblems, since many histories were efforts
to justify American nativist reactions to changing patterns
of immigration.[74] Thomas Clark has also hinted that the
local historian's greater familiarity with local history also
leads to opportunities to use more innovative sources and to
be in a position to determine what sources possess value for
continuing research.[75]

Archivists and manuscript curators have long been involved in efforts to collect textual and other sources documenting localities and regions. Ironically, the accumulation
and preservation of local historical manuscripts proceeded
in advance of those relating to the nation. Despite Jefferson's
interest in the preservation of historical documents, for
example, the problem with the care of his own papers
symbolizes the poverty of care for documents relating to
national history. As Merrill Peterson has pointed out,

> ...primary documents are the beginning of historical under-
> standing, but it was not until the end of the nineteenth
> century that American scholars made significant progress in
> the accumulation, verification, and analysis of the documen-
> tary record of the national life. The varied evidences of the
> movement in Jefferson historiography, almost without excep-
> tion, proved beneficial to his reputation. Jefferson's papers
> had been so badly managed—broken up, passed out as
> souvenirs, abandoned in private cabinets or entirely lost, and
> botched in editing—that the recovery and purification of the
> record was one of principal tasks of American scholarship.[76]

A long half-century fight for the creation of the National
Archives, along with failures in other national efforts to

preserve the records of the nation, possess similar patterns as that exhibited in the care of the Jefferson manuscripts.[77]

The development of archival and historical manuscript repositories has also been uniquely affected by a predisposition to the locality. State and local historical societies have long had a natural mandate to acquire and preserve the historical sources of localities. State government archives have acquired numerous sources of value to documenting the locality, as well as having been responsible for the nurturing of municipal, county, and town government archives. Business, religious, and other institutional archives have also been responsible for the preservation of many records necessary for understanding the locality. This impetus toward local historical sources is also supported by basic archival principles and theory, as most clearly annunciated by Canadian archivists.

> Already we have followed the basic principle that records should be retained and preserved by those responsible for creating them. In actual fact, of course, it is impractical to adhere rigidly to this principle, applying it to the great breadth of archival material ideally should be preserved. Thus it is necessary to emphasize the long-standing archival principle of *provenance,* namely, that records originating from the same source should be kept together and not interfiled with records from other sources. We should like to add to this old principle a new corollary to the effect that any particular set of records should remain, as far as possible, in the locale or milieu in which it was generated.[78]

Although this principle has not been universally accepted by North American archivists, it is nevertheless true that the challenges in preserving the documentary heritage will lead many archivists to accept such an operating precept. There is little question that the quantity of records and manuscripts possessing potential archival value is far too great either to be examined by archivists and their colleagues and, without question, far beyond the means of the collecting repositories such as colleges and universities, historical societies, and local libraries and museums.

It should be obvious that the concentration of archival records and historical manuscripts with potential value for local history research would be a stimulant to such research itself. The obviousness of this relationship can be seen in the many statements by historians about the importance of the archival and historical manuscripts repositories. An early summary of the important work of the 1960s and 1970s on the colonial Chesapeake region is but one example.

> The younger scholars...have increasingly taken on the appearance of a "school," with established centers of activity and with what may a times seem an unusual amount of interchange and interdependence in their work. So far as those who have worked primarily in Maryland are concerned, the centralization of Maryland records and the excellence of their management at the Hall of Records has played a part in the process. The St. Mary's City Commission, established to undertake an extensive and broadly defined study of Maryland's first capital, has generated extensive research by its own staff and has also emerged, along with the Hall of Records, where the commission's historians are based, as a center for the Chesapeake scholars. If the situation in Virginia, where research and archival activity is somewhat more dispersed and where there is a more numerous and older group of preservation agencies, has not been quite so concentrated, the Colonial Records Project, the opening of the extensive microform collections of the Colonial Williamsburg Foundation to visiting scholars, and the work of several important projects in historical archaeology, among other things, have nonetheless supplied something of the same focus for the work on that colony.[79]

The evidence of this natural relationship can be accumulated by the examination of the thousands of volumes of quite excellent local histories that have been published through the generations. But there are nagging questions remaining, of course, about certain aspects of this relationship.

While historians and other researchers become inspired by discoveries of caches of important documentation to undertake important local studies, there are still questions about the nature of the selection for preservation for such sources. Are these sources important because other, better sources have been lost or not discovered yet? What do all the sources add up in terms of any sort of adequacy of local documentation? Who has made the decisions for preservation of these sources, and what are the criteria for such decisions? These kinds of questions, many never really adequately answered, can plague the work of both archivists and their researchers. At this point in time, archivists have developed an interesting array of approaches to preserve the prime documentary sources of localities. But many of these approaches seem wanting in comparison to the larger question of whether we are actually adequately documenting the localities. The significance of the locality for understanding our past and present demands better and more systematic work than it seems we have provided.

NOTES

1. Michael L. Dertouzos, "Communications, Computers and Networks," *Scientific American* 265 (September 1991): 69.

2. *Electronic Language: A Philosophical Study of Word Processing* (New Haven: Yale University Press, 1987), p. 215.

3. *The Farther Shore: A Natural History of Perception, 1798-1984* (New York: Vintage Books, 1990), p. 193.

4. *Future Shock* (New York: Bantam Books, 1970), p. 92.

5. *The Age of Missing Information* (New York: Random House, 1992), pp. 22-23.

6. *Age of Missing Information,* p. 38.

7. *Understanding Media: The Extensions of Man* (New York: Mentor Books, 1964), p. 99.

8. See Cullen Murphy, "Force of Numbers: Demographics and Destiny," *The Atlantic* 270 (July 1992): 22.

9. Quoted in Carl N. Degler, *Out of Our Past: The Forces That Shaped Modern America* (New York: Harper & Brothers, 1959), pp. 43-44.

10. Thomas J. Schlereth, *Victorian America: Transformations in Everyday Life, 1876-1915* (New York: HarperPerennial Publishers, 1991), p. 152.

11. James Oliver Robertson, *American Myth American Reality* (New York: Hill and Wang, 1980), part three.

12. See, for example, Herbert W. Schneider, *A History of American Philosophy* (New York: Columbia University Press, 1946), pp. 144-59.

13. *Age of Missing Information,* pp. 40-41.

14. See especially chapter six in his *The Farther Shore.*

15. *The Opening of American Society: From the Adoption of the Constitution to the Eve of Disunion* (New York: Alfred A. Knopf, 1984), p. 282.

16. *City People: The Rise of Modern City Culture in Nineteenth-Century America* (New York: Oxford University Press, 1980), pp. 24-25.

17. See John F. Kasson, *Civilizing the Machine: Technology and Republican Values in America, 1776-1900* (New York: Penguin Books, 1976), chapter two.

18. Phil Patton, *Open Road: A Celebration of the American Highway* (New York: Simon and Schuster, 1986), pp. 20-21.

19. Richard B. Kielbowicz, *News in the Mail: The Press, Post Office, and Public Information, 1700-1860s,* Contributions in American History, no. 138, ed. Jon L. Wakelyn (Westport, CT: Greenwood Press, 1989) has this point of view. He writes for example, that "much of the printed mail—newspapers circulating outside their home town and the specialized journals of religion, reform, and occupational groups—represented supralocal communication. Using these publications, individuals in thousands of towns exchanged information and symbols....[P]ublic information circulating in the mails fostered the growth of overlapping communities, some complementary, others existing in a state of tension" (p. 67).

20. *The Experience of Place* (New York: Vintage Books, 1990), pp. 126-27.

21. *What Time Is This Place?* (Cambridge: MIT Press, 1972), p. 40.

22. See, for example, John Hanson Mitchell, *Ceremonial Time: Fifteen Thousand Years on One Square Mile* (Garden City, NY: Anchor Press/Doubleday, 1984) and John D. Dorst, *The Written Suburb: An American Site, An Ethnographic Dilemma* (Philadelphia: University of Pennsylvania Press, 1989).

23. Edgar B. Wesley, "History At Home," *Minnesota History* 19 (March 1938): 1. For similar views see Thomas D. Clark, "State and Local History, The Bedrock of Our Past," *East Tennessee History Society Publications* 48 (1976): 3-20; Robert M. Sutton, "After the Bicentennial and *Roots*: What Next? Local History at the Crossroads," in *Local History Today: Papers Presented at Four Regional Workshops for Local Historical Organizations in Indiania June 1978-April 1979* (Indianapolis: Indiana Historical Society, 1979), pp. 13-27.

24. U*sing Local History in the Classroom* (Nashville: American Association for State and Local History, 1982), p. 2.

25. *Nearby History: Exploring the Past Around You* (Nashville: American Association for State and Local History, 1982), p. 7.

26. *Towards A Better Understanding of History* (Notre Dame, IN: University of Notre Dame Press, 1960), p. 2.

27. See especially his *People of Paradox: An Inquiry Concerning the Origins of American Civilization* (New York: Alfred A. Knopf, 1973).

28. *On Doing Local History: Reflections on What Local Historians Do, Why, and What It Means* (Nashville: American Association for State and Local History, 1986), pp. 4-5.

29. *Families and Communities: A New View of American History* (Nashville: American Association for State and Local History, 1974), pp. 11-12.

30. "Community Study," *Historical Methods* 13 (Winter 1980): 31.

31. See diagrams 1:1b and 1:1c in Gerald A. Danzer and Lawrence W. McBride, *People, Space, and Time; The Chicago Neighborhood History Project: An Introduction to Community History for Schools* (Lanham, MD: Published for the Chicago Metro History Fair by the University Press of America, 1986).

32. "Americans, Mexicans, Metis: A Community Approach to the Comparative Study of North American Frontiers," in *Under An Open Sky: Rethinking America's Western Past*, eds. William Cronon, George Miles, and Jay Gitlin (New York: W. W. Norton and Co., 1992), p. 94.

33. See the classic essay on this topic by F. Gerald Ham, "The Archival Edge," *American Archivist* 38 (January 1975): 5-13.

34. "State and Local History," *Proceedings of the Mississippi Valley Historical Association* 10 (1920/21): 431.

35. Edward P. Alexander, "Getting the Most Out of Local History," *Michigan History Magazine* 29 (January/March 1945): 6.

36. *Keepers of Our Past: Local Historical Writing in the United States, 1820s-1930s* (New York: Greenwood Press, 1988).

37. "Local History or Ancestor Worship," *New England Social Studies Bulletin* 16 (1959): 19. See also essays such as Wesley, "History At Home."

38. "New Approaches to Local History," *Western Pennsylvania Historical Magazine* 55 (July 1972): 240.

39. "The Rising Place of Local and State History in American Historiography: A Personal Look at the Last Forty Years," *Locus* 1 (Fall 1988): 1. See also Carol Kammen's analysis of the work of the local historians predating and overlapping with the rise of the academic historian in *On Doing Local History*, chapter one.

40. "Community Studies, Urban History, and American Local History," in Michael Kammen, ed., *The Past Before Us: Contempo-*

rary Historical Writing in the United States (Ithaca, NY: Cornell University Press, 1980), p. 270.

41. "Community Studies," p. 222.

42. "Doing Local History: Monographic Approaches to the Smaller Community," *American Quarterly* 37, no. 3 (1985): 412-13.

43. "The Rising Place," p. 2.

44. "Local History and World Upheaval," *Minnesota History* 41 (Winter 1968): 174. For other statements similar to this, see Merrill E. Jarchow, "Exploring Local History: An Experience of 'Adventure, Anxiety, Exertion, and Success'," *Minnesota History* 39 (Fall 1965): 265-71.

45. For my views on this, see my "Genealogy and Public History: New Genealogical Guides and Their Implications for Public Historians," *Public Historian* 6 (Spring 1984): 89-96.

46. *Tradition and the Founding Fathers* (Charlottesville: University Press of Virginia, 1975), p. 54. Wright has provided a more detailed explanation of this view in his *The Cultural Life of the American Colonies 1607-1763* (New York: Harper and Row, 1957) and *Culture on the Moving Frontier* (Bloomington: Indiana University Press, 1955)

47. Max Lerner, *America As A Civilization: Life and Thought in the United States Today* (New York: Simon and Schuster, 1957), pp. 101-02.

48. "The Rising Place," p. 1. These, and other complaints, have been, of course, on target. Ann Douglas, for example, wrote

"The earliest historical research in America had been done at the local level, if only because...towns and states and sections were initially interested in history as a means of self-inflation and self-advertisement which could justify their claim to a bigger piece of the new national pie. In other words, the historical impulse in early nineteenth-century America was as natural to those who felt unjustly neglected as to those necessarily involved in the problem of conspicuousness. The men and women who wrote local, antiquarian, or biographical history at this time were fascinated by the meaning of obscurity....These chroniclers discovered their mission in redeeming what was discounted as waste by imperialist Hegelian history, and in many ways their effort was potentially admirable and farsighted" (*The Feminization of American Culture,* New York: Discus Book, 1977, pp. 217-18).

49. Earl Spangler, "Study and Research in Local and State History," *Social Studies* 57 (October 1966): 208-13; Charlton W. Tebeau, "History Is Where You Find It," *West Virginia History* 34 (July 1968): 278-82; Ralph W. Cordier, "The Study of History

Through State and Local Resources," *Social Studies* 60 (March 1969): 99-104; Roger K. Warlick, "The History Lab: Methodology Through Enquiry," *New England Social Studies Bulletin* 34 (1976/77): 27-32.

50. Occasionally, professional historians have pointed out the similarity in problems with their own work with that of their amateur colleagues. Robert Dykstra was one of these academics, noting that

"the local history taboo on social conflict comes down to us from nineteenth-century amateur writing, but professional scholarship perpetuates it. Historians of American urbanism, for example, insofar as they have produced 'city biographies,' or case studies of successful urbanization, write in much the same vein. Like the local historian, the city biographer makes progress his controlling theme. He assumes that it occurred only within the context of community harmony. He views occasional conflicts as disturbing social aberrations to be overcome before further progress could take place. He feels called upon to apologize for them as embarrassing instances of urban immaturity" (*The Cattle Towns*, New York: Atheneum, 1974, p. 364).

51. "America's Heritage," *New York History* 36 (April 1955): 130.

52. "America's Heritage," pp. 133-34.

53. "Local History: A Mainspring for National History," in *Local History Today: Papers Presented at Four Regional Workshops for Local Historical Organization in Indiana June 1978 - April 1979* (Indianapolis: Indiana Historical Society, 1979), p. 31.

54. *The Classical Foundations of Modern Historiography* (Berkeley: University of California Press, 1990), p. 54.

55. "History From Below," in *New Perspectives on Historical Writing,* ed. Peter Burke (University Park: Pennsylvania State University Press, 1991), p. 36.

56. *Keepers of Our Past,* p. 203.

57. "Doing Local History," p. 413.

58. "Doing Local History," p. 6.

59. See, for example, Samuel P. Hays, ed., *City at the Point: Essays on the Social History of Pittsburgh* (Pittsburgh: University of Pittsburgh, 1989) and the review of this book by John Rowett, "Pittsburgh Anatomized," *Pittsburgh History* 74 (Fall 1991): 127-40.

60. Quoted in Richard Beale Davis, *Literature and Society in Early Virginia 1608-1840* (Baton Rouge: Louisiana State University Press, 1973), p. 194.

61. Davis, *Literature and Society in Early Virginia,* p. 232.

62. Russel Blaine Nye, *The Cultural Life of the New Nation, 1776-1830* (New York: Harper Torchbook, 1963), pp. 42-43; Nye, *Society and Culture in America, 1830-1860* (New York: Harper Torchbook, 1974), pp. 101-14.

63. Quoted in H. G. Jones, *For History's Sake: The Preservation and Publication of North Carolina History 1663-1903* (Chapel Hill: University of North Carolina Press, 1966), p. 243.

64. See, for example, Richard J. Cox, "A Century of Frustration: The Movement for a State Archives in Maryland, 1811-1935," *Maryland Historical Magazine* 78 (1983): 106-17 and "The Origins of American Religious Archives: Ethan Allen, Pioneer Church Historian and Archivist of Maryland," *Journal of the Canadian Church Historical Society* 29 (1987): 48-63.

65. *History in the United States 1800-1860: Its Practice and Purpose* (Baltimore, MD: Johns Hopkins Press, 1970), p. 115.

66. For example, Max Savelle in a pioneering analysis of the foundations of an "American" mind carefully discussed early efforts at local and regional historical research and writing but reserved his highest praise for one history because it "was by far the most remarkable of them all, for not only was it thoroughly secular in outlook and built upon a genuine effort to get the facts...but—and this was it most remarkable feature—it set out to be a history of all the colonies as a whole" (p. 382). While it is possible that Savelle's comments were framed in the way that they were because of the topic of his study, they also reflectged a predilection by academic historians of that period (the time Savelle was writing) to put national history on a higher plane than the local and regional variety *(Seeds of Liberty: The Genesis of the American Mind,* Seattle: University of Washington Press, 1965, pp. 376-85). This is certainly the theme of David Russo's *Keepers of Our Past.*

67. R. W. B. Lewis, *The American Adam: Innocence, Tragedy and Tradition in the Nineteenth Century* (Chicago: University of Chicago Press, 1955), chapter 8; Henry Steele Commager, *The American Mind: An Interpretation of American Thought and Character Since the 1880's* (New Haven, CT: Yale University Press, 1954), chapters 13 and 14.

68. *Reflections on History and Historians* (Madison: University of Wisconsin Press, 1987), p. 13.

69. Clarke Thomas, "Making a Place for History," *Pittsburgh Post-Gazette,* 31 July 1991.

70. *Rockdale: The Growth of an American Village in the Early Industrial Revolution* (New York: Alfred A. Knopf, 1978), p. 473.

71. Quoted in Leslie W. Dunlap, *American Historical Societies 1790-1860* (Madison, WI: Privately printed, 1944), p. 65.

72. "Putting the Past under Glass: Preservation and the Idea of History in the Mid-Nineteenth Century," *Prospects* 10 (1985): 259-60.

73. *No Place of Grace: Antimodernism and the Transformation of American Culture 1880-1920* (New York: Pantheon Books, 1981), p. 188.

74. John Higham, *Strangers in the Land: Patterns of American Nativism 1860-1925* (New York: Atheneum, 1970).

75. "Local History," p. 43.

76. *The Jefferson Image in the American Mind* (New York: Oxford University Press, 1960), pp. 308-09.

77. See, for example, Victor Gondos, Jr., *J. Franklin Jameson and the Birth of the National Archives 1906-1926* (Philadelphia: University of Pennsylvania Press, 1981).

78. Consultative Group on Canadian Archives, *Canadian Archives: Report to the Social Sciences and Humanities Research Council of Canada* (Ottawa: Social Sciences and Humanities Research Council of Canada, 1980), pp. 15-16.

79. Thad W. Tate, "The Seventeenth-Century Chesapeake and Its Modern Historians," in *The Chesapeake in the Seventeenth Century: Essays on Anglo-American Society,* eds. Thad W. Tate and David L. Ammerman (New York: W. W. Norton and Company for the Institute of Early American History and Culture in Williamsburg, Virginia, 1979), p. 44.

2

DOCUMENTING LOCALITIES: TRADITIONAL APPROACHES

A COLLECTING PREOCCUPATION

In the first chapter we saw how the geographical locality has maintained a persistent importance for both historical researchers (antiquarian, amateur, and professional) and archivists and manuscript curators. The focus of that chapter was on how the locality has been significant for every American and, as well, how researchers' interest in localities has driven (to a very great extent) the work of archivists and manuscript curators in the United States. There is a demand for local sources, and the repositories have been developed to house the records, manuscripts, and other documentary materials. This chapter intends to examine in greater detail how American archivists and their colleagues have pursued their basic appraisal, acquisition, and documentation efforts in the light of this strong local orientation.

A few comments are in order as a way of providing some context for this topic and stating what will be considered throughout the remainder of this book. There is little question that the historical manuscripts tradition—that is, the "collecting" emphasis—has been the primary source for thinking about and conducting archival appraisal in the United States. While the terminology of "values" (evidential

and informational) have been adopted from the public archives tradition, primarily the writings of T. R. Schellenberg,[1] their use has been uneven and modified for the
acquisition of archives and manuscripts by all types of
archival and historical manuscript repositories. The oft-
quoted statement by Richard Berner that his book on archival theory was not addressing appraisal theory is possibly
the main outcome of the collecting stress by American
archivists.[2] It has only recently been with the work of
individuals such as Hans Booms, Terry Cook, and Helen
Samuels that the collecting preoccupation has been sufficiently overcome (in theory, at least—practice is still another
matter) and a real archival appraisal theory begun to develop.[3]

The impact of this focus on appraisal is even more evident
through the commentaries of foreign archivists, with different philosophical and theoretical orientations as well as
different political and cultural environments, on the practice
of American archivists. Australian archivist Glenda Acland
has stated that "archival institutions in the 1990s should
not be acquisition driven or custody oriented nor managed
primarily as information outlets."[4] Acland's statement is
certainly counter to the acquisition/collecting mentality of
most American archivists. Dutch archivist Joan Van Albada
has been more to the point concerning American archival
practice. Based on attendance at Society of American Archivists meetings, he stated that "most sessions, apart from
those related to topics like conservation and user services,
dealt with collecting and documenting and not with the core
of the profession: archives management, the accessioning,
selection and appraisal, and processing of record groups."[5]
Canadian archivist Terry Cook has provided yet another
important perspective. He has noted that archivists have
tended to fixate on the wrong things: "Rather than address
these broader contextual issues, however, archivists have
tended to concentrate their appraisal activities on the resulting end-product—the actual record—and the potential possibly evident in it for actual or anticipated research."[6] Such
preoccupations are a direct result of the collecting mentality
of American archivists. While Cook sees issues of documen-

tation as essential, he strongly shows how theory and new strategies and methodologies have been stillborn in the acquisition frenzy, often reactive, of most archival programs. This is why Susan Grigg, writing advice for historians' use of archives, noted that "an evolutionary view of archives and manuscript repositories is as essential to search method as a genetic understanding of the sources themselves. This is because the growth of their collections has been as much a historical process as the events they document and the scholarship they foster." Grigg then briefly describes the various means by which such programs have developed.[7]

These kinds of concerns will be addressed directly in this chapter in an analysis of the approaches followed by American archivists in their appraisal work. Thus, this chapter is more a description of present practice and an introduction to the archival documentation strategy concept that this author advocates as an approach needing more serious attention, certainly as a partial remedy for dealing with some of the problems now facing appraisal practice. Following this will be case studies on the use of the archival documentation strategy, and a description of a methodology for the use of the archival documentation strategy in documenting localities. An analysis of appraisal theory in the light of newer approaches such as the documentation strategy was not included in this volume so as not to detract attention from the practical application of this approach.

THE FRAGILITY OF LOCAL ARCHIVES AND HISTORICAL DOCUMENTATION AS A COLLECTING RATIONALE

There should be little question that one of the characteristics of local documentation that inspires archivists and manuscripts curators to acquire it is its ephemeral nature. The material remains (manuscript, artifactual, or whatever) of our past are extremely fragile, instilling a variety of fears in both archivists/manuscript curators and their researcher patrons (see Figure 2-1). In 1931, Lewis Mumford lamented that we had already destroyed much of the architecture and art created only fifty years before: "In our haste to remove the debris, unfortunately, we have already destroyed much

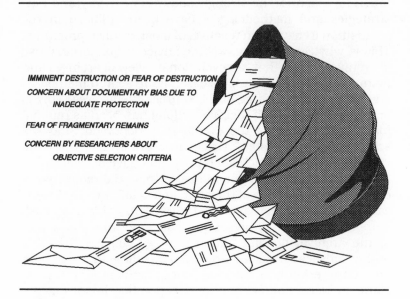

IMMINENT DESTRUCTION OR FEAR OF DESTRUCTION
CONCERN ABOUT DOCUMENTARY BIAS DUE TO
    INADEQUATE PROTECTION

FEAR OF FRAGMENTARY REMAINS

CONCERN BY RESEARCHERS ABOUT
    OBJECTIVE SELECTION CRITERIA

Figure 2-1. Fragility as a Cause for Collecting

that was precious in the Brown Decades; and unless we rapidly recover a little common sense we shall doubtless destroy much more."[8] It seems that local history sources, in particular, are also endangered, perhaps even more so than the architectural elements described by Mumford. Carol Kammen related this story about their fragility.

[A local historian] reports that in his village for many years town meetings were held upstairs over a local hardware store. When town officials moved to new quarters, the old books and records were left behind in the attic. It was not believed that they were particularly useful documents, and no one gave them much thought. They had, after all, been safe in the hardware store for over one hundred years. A new owner of the hardware company, however, hired some local boys to remove the debris from the building, and during that cleanup they took the accumulated clutter to the town dump. There they poured gas on the old papers and set the pile afire. Town residents recall that for weeks afterwards scraps of burned ledger paper could be picked up along the main road.[9]

Such examples abound, and every archivist and manuscript curator can recount stories such as this. Lyman Butterfield's example of the use of seventeenth-century Boston town records to serve as steampipe insulation is only too typical of what has happened with the historical records of our localities. After describing a century and a half of strenuous activities by Bostonians to preserve their historical records, Butterfield still had to admit that the public archival records were in pitiful condition.

> The early records still housed in the old courthouse building present a sorry contrast. It is sometimes difficult for an inquirer there to consult again what has been consulted before, and I have been in a basement storage room where one must literally walk on old papers covered with dust, soot, and plaster grit in order to reach materials jammed helter-skelter into the shelves.[10]

Twenty years later, a series of reports issued by various State Historical Records Advisory Boards featured numerous examples similar to what Butterfield had described in his essay. In Alabama's 1985 report, for example, the following showed the nature of the neglect.

> The condition of many of Alabama's local records is appalling. ...One concerned resident and amateur historian wrote in desperation to the state archives declaring that the records in the state's courthouses in north Alabama were literally being carried off. ...Records of another Alabama county recently showed up at a flea market in New Jersey, the result of a county employee having removed and sold them. Yet another county, in an effort to raise money to purchase band uniforms, even considered auctioning off the old public records for this purpose.[11]

While such examples can be blamed on public and government neglect and ignorance or the lack of knowledge of civil servants, they do, as well, demonstrate the general fragility of the local documentary heritage. This fragility often compels individuals and institutions to collect documentary materials they perceive to be in imminent danger, sometimes irregardless of their perceived potential value.

The fragility of the recorded past has prompted two other viewpoints pertinent to this study. First, scholarly historians have recognized the fragmentary nature of surviving documentation, written and otherwise. Henry Steele Commager, among many, has stated that the

> record is not only irremediably incomplete, it is also lopsided and biased....Much of it is wholly fortuitous. Our knowledge of the past depends pretty much on what happened to be preserved, and what happened to be preserved is only a minute part of the total record, minute and indiscriminate....There is no logic here, no pattern; what has survived is largely a matter of luck.
>
> Largely—but not wholly; for what has survived—or rather what has failed to survive—is also to some degree a matter of power....
>
> The record which has come down to us, then, is not only fragmentary and selective, it is also biased.[12]

The events in Boston and Alabama certainly seem to agree with such an assessment.

But, there is a second, and more serious, problem. This historical view toward documentation has prompted archivists to worry about their objectivity and to shy away from careful appraisal planning and selection criteria and theory, a perspective which only exacerbates the kind of problem Commager, Butterfield, and others have commented upon. Some historians and other researchers have worried about appraisal by the records creators and custodians such as archivists. Gwyn Prins, for example, wrote that the "volume of official paper has cascaded beyond control. There has to be selection for preservation, so the 'weeders' have also been systematically at work, and therefore what official archives contain may, either by conscious, usually mischievous, intent or by virtue of wrong choices in what to preserve and what to burn, be quite as misleading as other sources."[13] Unless archivists become systematic in their appraisal of local sources and more advanced in their approaches to documenting localities, such concerns will be openly expressed. Instead, it sometimes seems that archivists and their colleagues hasten to acquire nearly any and all documentary remnants in the fear that they might be lost or some potential researcher deprived of their use, when, instead, they should develop a specific mechanism for determining when such records should be acquired and preserved.

Many of the values attributed to the work of local historians are relevant for the institutional archivist and the archivists and manuscript curators involved in the historical societies, museums, colleges and universities, and other similar repositories. In 1938, one historian listed the attributes of local history as being that of

- Making the community intelligible.
- Creating an interest in and a love for one's own community.
- Understanding state, national, and world affairs.
- Assisting the understanding [of] the whole field of history.
- Its utility as a standard of selecting other history.
- Protecting one against current events—providing the "basis for an appraisal" of such events so that the "ephemeral" is not mistaken "for the enduring."[14]

Local archives and other locally oriented institutions such as museums and libraries possess similar agendas. Gaynor Kavanagh, writing from the English perspective, noted that the "museum has the potential and the capacity for touching the quick of local, human experience and for offering stunning and challenging insights into a personal and very human past."[15] The sources, many untapped, residing in local archives and manuscript repositories, possess the same potential.

The physical fragility of these sources and the potential for a skewing of the documentary heritage through haphazard or careless appraisal practices both challenge the vitality and viability of the value of local history sources. The physical problems can be handled, although not necessarily easily so, by a combination of resources, appropriate staff and user education, and good preservation management principles and practices. But adopting, developing, and fine-tuning appraisal methodologies and practices is a far different type of challenge. New archival appraisal approaches requires a serious directional shift in the intellectual foundations of archival work; it is not a question just of better technique and new resources, but the transformation of an archival culture that has been dominant, at least in the United States, for the better part of the twentieth century.

Pushing back the dominant archival culture and opening up new frontiers of thinking has been difficult, at least as evident from the archival writings of the past decade. F. Gerald Ham, in a series of essays published between 1975 and 1983, tried to get the American archival profession to move from a custodial to a postcustodial mentality, that is, from a discipline less defined by the records and more the shapers of the documentary sources they possess.[16] While his arguments were convincing, it is equally evident that there have been minimal changes in archival appraisal practice. David Bearman's major contribution was his series of essays gathered in *Archival Methods* in 1989, a dramatic portrayal of the fact that present archival practice is extremely unrealistic in light of the reality of modern documentation.[17] While Bearman's radical suggestions were being presented to the profession, a major analysis of archival appraisal practice was being conducted; the upshot of this study was an elaborate evaluation of selection criteria that nearly returned archivists to the task of analyzing every file.[18] It seems that the archival profession still had not come very far in its thinking about basic approaches to archival appraisal, a topic which will be the focus of this chapter.

PROBLEMS OF PRESENT APPROACHES TO THE SELECTION OF LOCAL HISTORY MATERIALS

There are many barriers obstructing the selection of local historical sources (see Table 2-1). The primary problem that confronts any institution interested in preserving the past of a locality, whether it is stressing archival or other materials, is the manner in which that institution determines what its task really is about. Oral historian Linda Shopes has articu-

Table 2-1: Present Archival Selection Approaches and Their Problems for Local Documentation

APPROACH	PROBLEM
Identification of Acquisition Mission	Determining Realistic Scope
Documenting Locality	Definition of Locality; Lack of Institutional Archives; Lack of Repository Cooperation
Appraisal Criteria	Subjectivity; Lack of Definition and Measurable Objectives
Interdisciplinary Coordination and Cooperation	Lack of Experience; Perceived Costs; Leadership Needs

lated this concern when considering local history projects and the place of oral history.

> The question becomes: how to take community oral history projects beyond trivia and nostalgia? How to infuse them with conflict, change, action, direction?...[T]he various manuals available to us offer little insight. Though they present excellent advice on the techniques of doing research, they avoid more fundamental questions about the purposes of such inquiries in the first place; they suggest long lists of topics for investigation, but don't challenge us to define the questions, the perspectives that shape the choice of topics in the first place; they describe how to create a slide show, a publication, but don't confront problems of interpretation, don't explain how any historical production necessarily provides an interpretation of the data presented.[19]

The problem Shopes described is a common one for local history organizations and individuals interested in local history. A half-century ago, Edward Alexander argued that a local historical society should possess "a five-year plan for research and collection." Alexander noted that "it is always difficult to determine what a library or museum should collect, and too much collection is haphazard, governed only by what is offered and by attempts to please donors. An outline of the history of a community will suggest fields for collection which can be actively pursued."[20] While there are problems, such as these, the locality provides the means for a focus, as Kavanagh has suggested for history museums.

> The notion of "community" is a useful means of identifying common interest and concerns: their manifestations, contradictions and changes. It can be used in all history museums as, regardless of degrees of wealth or location, the social nature of our existence creates bonds through common interests. Whereas not all societies are communities, all communities are societies, with distinct cultural norms and values. They provide the fine and sometimes definitive textures to our means of social being. Through community studies, ways of organizing, interpreting and comparing data can be developed.[21]

To a certain extent archivists and manuscript curators have developed a concept of community or locality as well, but acquisitiveness and a general lack of appraisal standards have overridden the potential of building conceptual frameworks for conducting appraisal and documenting localities.

Archival and historical manuscript repositories can also develop some sound selection criteria or strategies because of their local orientation, not far removed from the advice James H. Conrad gave to community libraries contemplating local history programs: "A combination of geographical and political boundaries define the collection area for the library, which will probably be the same as the library's service area, though not necessarily."[22] A state government archives staff member summarized this challenge quite well in the late 1970s.

> Collecting, in the strictest definition of the term, is not the first order of business in preserving local historical resources. The basis, the foundation, the *sine qua non*, the bottom line of any preservation program, is the identification of culturally

significant resources. Obviously, before a historical resource can be collected or singled out for preservation, it must first be identified. And, ideally, the decision on what to collect and preserve should not be made until all cultural resources in a particular locale are identified. It is impossible for any local group to preserve every historical resource—every building, every site, every document, every photograph, every artifact— in a given locale. It is, simply, not possible physically.[23]

One of the major weaknesses in American archival work in the last several generations, for example, has been the lack of development of certain kinds of institutional archives, such as those represented in large and important business and financial corporations. It is very possible that the American archival community's desire to collect or acquire has worked against the development of such archives and, consequentially, made the aim to document localities in any logical manner nearly impossible to meet.[24]

Many suggestions have been made to resolve this problem of focus and related concerns. Shopes argued for a "problem-centered approach to community oral history projects" in which they "shape their inquiry as an effort to understand some problem facing the community, a problem with contemporary significance but historical roots—and future ramifications."[25] Others have come up with similar structural approaches. Mark Friedberger and Janice Reiff Webster have argued that the

> central theme around which community studies might be successfully organized is what the technical literature calls "social structure." At its broadest, social structure includes each of the elements (persons and groups) within a society and the interaction of those elements. More specifically, social structure is concerned with the hierarchical relationships within a community, the distribution of power and goods, and the educational, religious, ethnic, demographic, and political identification of its residents.[26]

Friedberger and Webster proposed this approach due to their perception that "local history [was] a field...without a conceptual framework or a workable methodology."[27] Others have come up with far more simple explanations. Conrad suggested that

> the primary purpose of the local history collection is straight-forward: to preserve source information on the history of the local community and make the material available to library patrons and researchers. The rationale is simple: if the library or local historical society does not collect such materials, who will?[28]

Conrad also noted that these collections should be "compre-hensive."[29]

It is one thing to establish collecting or selecting parameters, a major activity which has generated tremendous discussion and activity within the archival profession, but the bigger challenge is the subjectivity of selection criteria. One state archives administrator has noted that "there are no absolute standards of value for what we choose to collect and preserve. Historical significance, as we all know, is relative. Since we cannot preserve everything, we must of necessity be selective."[30] It is in this realm that we enter into the matter of what adequate documentation is meant to be. We can take the lead of the work of the National Archives, that defined this concept in this manner:

> *Adequate and proper documentation* means a record of the conduct of Government business that is complete and accurate to the extent required to document the organization, functions, policies, decisions, procedures, and essential transactions of the agency and that is designed to furnish the information necessary to protect the legal and financial rights of the Government and of persons directly affected by the agency's activities.[31]

It is not difficult to substitute "locality" or "community" for government in this statement in order to develop a concept for adequate local documentation. How anyone achieves such "adequate and proper" documentation is, of course, a completely different matter. And the general resistance of most American archivists to use models or frameworks has made this kind of work even more difficult.

Individuals concerned with geographical localities have certainly puzzled over such matters. Local historians and archivists and manuscripts curators are also aware of the many gaps in their own work. Thomas Clark has noted that "in spite of the fact that row upon row of library stacks bear thousands of localized books, gaps in this kind of history are incalculable. With little effort any historian familiar with a region could compile an extensive list of subjects which should be investigated."[32] Such gaps have occurred at least partly because of weaknesses in the thoroughness of local documentation. In other words, despite many different techniques and long, hard efforts on the part of archivists and manuscript curators with an eye to the thorough documentation of localities, the success of accomplishing such documentation has been elusive.

The elusiveness of the quest for ensuring adequate documentation of local geographic regions may seem to be an unusual problem in light of the immense quantity of repositories with an emphasis on this goal. A scanning of local, state, regional, and national directories to archives and manuscripts repositories will reveal that many areas, especially urban centers (see chapter 4), possess clusters of historical societies, libraries with local history programs, colleges and universities that both collect thematically and seek to document their own organizations, and institutional archives of all shapes and sizes. But this is not a phenomenon restricted to citified localities. Walter Muir Whitehall's classic study on historical societies in the early 1960s made a valiant effort to describe the nature and diversity of the kinds of local manuscript repositories that have developed. As he stated, the "greater part of local historical societies owe their origin to the interest and devotion of people on the spot who genuinely care for the characteristics of their region."[33] Or, in another comment, Whitehill noted that "no general listing will ever give the full picture of the scattered documents that have found homes in unlikely places."[34] The ubiquitousness of such local repositories has been confirmed again and again in subsequent studies and reports.[35]

There are many reasons why documentary gaps have appeared despite the large number of locally oriented archival and historical manuscripts programs. One reason has been the general lack of cooperative efforts. Canadian archivists have noted that, "in theory, there should be no competition among archives," although the difficulty in minimizing competition also prompted the Canadians to foster the notion of "total archives"—"archives which...actively acquire both the unofficial records and an extensive range of private materials in all documentary media bearing on the life of their institution or region."[36] Cooperation of any real extent simply has not developed in American archives, except in certain functions (like descriptive standards) which quickly proved their value to the work of specific institutions.

Another reason for local documentary gaps is the difficulty of coming to grips with what a locality or a region actually encompasses. Historian Leland Baldwin commenced his analysis of America's meaning with a description of this nation's diversity. "Modern regionalism," he noted,

> fosters certain cultural, social, and economic unities but it does not aspire to isolation or independence; it does not even aspire actively to administrative unity or autonomy, and sometimes there is not even a focal metropolitan center—or there may be two or three. It has a certain amount of geographic and climatic unity, but these must not be over-stressed, for there is a great deal of internal variety. The nebulous nature of regional character is evidenced by the way in which writers on the subject differ from each other in the boundaries they draw between regions. The best guide, perhaps, is found in the local *feeling* of homogeneity, and this results from psychological and historical factors as well as from authentic cultural, economic, geographical, and climatic factors. But like factors may play entirely different roles in different regions—and all factors must be assessed with care. It must also be borne in mind that there are binding as well as separating factors. The effect of a common political and economic federalism is obvious. No less clear is the effect of the scores of privately-run national organizations which bring together businessmen, laborers, farmers, educators, churchmen, reformers, and veterans.[37]

Some of the opposition to using archival methodologies like the documentation strategy has developed because of initial difficulties in defining a region or locality, a topic or theme, or an ongoing trend or long-term and significant event. As will be discussed in subsequent chapters, it is possible to develop working definitions which can be used in successful cooperative efforts. Working definitions of geographic areas can be used and, more importantly, refined as necessary and strengthened as appraisal and documentation analysis proceeds. At the least, such flawed beginning definitions are, in many cases, better than reactive collecting without clear objectives or appraisal without broader documentary objectives.

There is also a strong impetus that archivists should open up the process that they use for appraising and acquiring the records and manuscripts that supposedly document localities. For one thing, archivists have learned from historians how certain sources should be used and, as well, have seen the demands for their records change to reflect new developments in local and community history research. One of the main contributions of historian Merle Curti's 1959 *The Making of an American Community: A Case Study of Democracy in a Frontier County* was that

> it introduced a major advance in historical method. Previously, a few scholars had used the United States manuscript census schedules as a primary historical source. Curti showed how this rich but vast mass of data on individual lives could be manipulated to yield broad and convincing generalizations. His use of statistical methods, nominal record linkage, punch card processing, and calculating machines to reveal hidden structures of social and economic life represented an enormous methodological contribution.[38]

Not surprisingly, many archivists have laid tribute at the feet of the pioneering social historians and, furthermore, used their studies to develop new or to expand existing collecting and appraisal strategies. Fredric Miller, as just one example, used the work of social historians to inform archivists about changes they should make in appraisal and acquisition.[39]

The matter of the archivist's role in society, from the perspective of the selection of what records should be preserved, has also long been a matter of discussion by the archival community. Some have argued that the archivist's role is to assist institutions to identify what has continuing evidential value for them, while others have stressed broader documentary roles. Luciana Duranti, serving as the closing speaker at the 1991 Association of Canadian Archivists meeting focused on archival appraisal theory and practice, struck an interesting perspective in trying to bring these two divergent views together.

> What if, rather than considering the archivist the professional responsible for the formation of the cultural heritage, the "documenter" of society, we look at this professional as the mediator between social forces and the people, between the records creators and those for whom the records are created in the first place? What if we see the archivist as the societal officer responsible for maintaining the essential values of his or her society by preserving the evidence of its actions and transactions? The formation of a cultural heritage would undoubtedly be a consequence of the archivist's endeavour, but not its main purpose. Its main purpose would be the identification and preservation of what guarantees the survival and development of the socio-political-juridical system in which the archivist lives.[40]

The need to bring such perspectives and principles together can be seen in the various approaches archivists have developed and described for preserving the archives and historical manuscripts of localities. In fact, Frederick Stielow, in an effort to develop an archival theory, has laid down as one of two fundamental principles the "Stewardship Principle": "Archivists have responsibilities to take material in their charge and to insure the development of a documentary heritage from these."[41] This is an excellent principle to keep in mind as we review the appraisal and acquisition approaches used by archivists in the United States. What follows is a description of the methodology and practice aspects of archival appraisal science as used on the local level; the theoretical dimensions will be more fully considered in the next chapter.

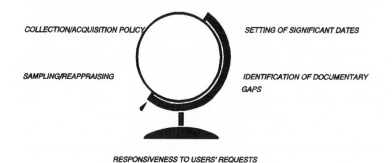

COLLECTION/ACQUISITION POLICY

SAMPLING/REAPPRAISING

SETTING OF SIGNIFICANT DATES

IDENTIFICATION OF DOCUMENTARY
GAPS

RESPONSIVENESS TO USERS' REQUESTS

Figure 2-2. Traditional Approaches to Documenting Localities

TRADITIONAL APPROACHES TO DOCUMENTING LOCALITIES: A SUMMARY AND CRITIQUE

Archivists and manuscript curators, working in institutions such as historical societies and universities and colleges possessing local orientations, have developed many approaches to documenting localities (see Figure 2-2). Many of these approaches have emerged as a result of practical concerns such as shortages of resources or institutional mandates and traditions rather than broad theoretical principles or professional missions and objectives. In fact, it is probably correct to say that practical aims have been far more important than broader theoretical or professional objectives, despite the fact that the right models and frameworks could help archivists to use their resources more efficiently and effectively. In a very clear sense, these have developed in an ad hoc fashion and they have contributed to the general problems on inadequate documentation of localities.

For collecting repositories such as historical societies, public libraries, and historic sites and museums, the most essential approach seems to have been the use and development of the collecting or acquisition policy. Faye Phillips'

1984 essay on formulating manuscript collecting policies has remained the most usable statement of what this device is and how it should be used. After a lengthy review of why such policies are important and what archivists and manuscript curators have had to say about them, Phillips defines the policy as a statement assisting such professionals to work toward written acquisition or documentary goals and then provides a clear, utilitarian template for the composition of such policies. In her view, such policies should include statements on the purpose, programmatic forms supported by the collection, research clientele served by the collection, specific statements on the priorities and limitations of the collecting program, cooperative agreements which may affect the policy, resource sharing, deaccessioning, and procedures (including a process for monitoring the collecting policy's use and relevance).[42] What we possess is a useful concept and an even more useful model. Any manuscripts repository which would use this as a starting point could develop an excellent conceptual platform for the acquisition of manuscripts.

The utility of the collecting or acquisition policy is well demonstrated in F. Gerald Ham's recent appraisal primer in the Archival Fundamental Series of the Society of American Archivists. Ham refers to the policy as a "framework" for selection and as an "essential" guide to appraisal and acquisition. It also can be seen to be an important foundation for all appraisal work. Ham also wisely expands the notion to be valuable as a tool to be used by institutional archives and adds the notion of a tool (collection analysis) which can be used for evaluating the effectiveness of the acquisition policy. Like Philips, Ham defines and describes the elements of the policy and provides examples of working policies.[43]

There can be little question that the acquisition policy is essential for institutions operating with a mandate to document all or a portion of a locality. The acquisition policy can be used to define precisely what aspects of the locality should be in the purview of the repository's work. It is the basis of determining success in such documentation efforts, providing a benchmark or point for measure regarding how well an institution is doing in its appraisal/acquisition mission. It is also essential for developing a basis for cooperation in documentation. No single repository can document all aspects of a geographic region, but the process of determining collection priorities can (and should be) used for identifying areas where other repositories are working, noting existing or potential institutional archives, and ascertaining where new appraisal or acquisition strategies can be used. Acquisition policies can even be effectively used by institutional archives to state their own documentary goals and to define their place and responsibility in their geographic settings.[44]

There is little question that the acquisition policy, developed by archives and historical manuscripts repositories, is the most important cog in the development of approaches to documenting localities. It is also apparent that creating such policies is a difficult task for a number of reasons. What are the obstacles to writing such policies and, then, using them in practical ways? There are, in most geographic areas, too few repositories to care for in any meaningful way the range and volume of documentation. This often works against the inclination of these institutions, especially historical societies, to ensure that every document with value is saved for posterity. Moreover, such local repositories are often ensconced in strong antiquarian traditions from the nineteenth century prompting them to want to save everything of documentary value and, it must be said, curiosity.

Other problems weigh down these local repositories in their efforts to craft meaningful and useful acquisition policies. They are often underfunded and lack adequate professional staff, and these programs see themselves as too burdened to stop and expend resources on such activities as planning and policy development when they are hard-pressed to keep up with daily responsibilities. This often causes such programs to become only reactive—we will deal with a set of records when they are offered, become known to us, or are endangered—or, and just as bad, eliminates their ability to be more self-reflective and to ask the right kinds of questions about what aspects of a locality should be documented. Because of tradition or other priorities, many of the locally oriented archival and historical manuscript programs see themselves in a noncooperative light;

that is, they either tend to perceive themselves as solely responsible for the documentation of a locality or, and much worse, they seriously compete with other programs for prize or jewel collections and fonds. Such attitudes often undermine any efforts to develop useful acquisition policies or to develop practical strategies for such activities as documenting localities.

So, what is the impact of these obstacles on the traditional and commonly accepted approaches, primarily the acquisition policy, to documenting geographic regions? There is a very broad spectrum of effects. On one hand, many local repositories have not developed acquisition policies in any form. A decade ago, for example, an analysis of historical records programs in New York state had the following comments in this area.

> Most repositories in the State have not developed careful policies that clearly indicate the types of records they collect. Without settled collections strategies, they build up their holdings haphazardly and unsystematically. Moreover, few historical records repositories communicate or cooperate with each other on an ongoing basis, and repositories have generally not worked together to develop local, regional, or statewide documentation strategies. Historical records programs sometimes compete with or wastefully duplicate each other's efforts. There is great variation in the quality and adequacy of programs among repositories in the State. No ongoing means exist for collecting and analyzing data on a statewide basis regarding collecting patterns and trends.[45]

Such patterns have been confirmed in other states as well.[46] On the other hand, there have been many institutions which have adopted written statements for acquisition which lack specificity. One regional historical society, for example, has developed special collecting emphases on specific ethnic groups, each one with the following kind of mission statement: "The purpose of the Slovak-American Collection of Western Pennsylvania is to collect, maintain and provide access to materials relating to Western Pennsylvania's important Slovak-American community." While the intention of such efforts are certainly good, the implication is that anything interesting or curious as well as important will be acceptable; in other words there is no discernible criteria here for acquisition or documentation.[47] The end-result is a lack of proper perspective on their tasks of acquiring archives and historical manuscripts which, in turn, undermine the ability to see what present holdings and prospective acquisitions (all the other documentation not in the repositories) add up to and whether they are meeting any stated goals. Even a well-known and excellent institution, after being engaged in an evaluation of its holdings, determined that the auto industry should be a priority for collecting because of its "enormous size, its economic importance, the hostility of the industry to outside researchers, and the limited number of significant repository holdings."[48] This priority should not be the focus of any single collecting repository; rather, it should be a target for interinstitutional cooperation and concerted efforts to develop viable institutional archives.

There have been other problems as well. Archivists have tended to adopt principles for appraisal and selection that are driven by the records themselves rather than any other documentary objectives. The classic statement of this approach appeared in Maynard Brichford's 1977 basic manual on appraisal.

> Records appraisal is best considered as a *process* that requires extensive staff preparation, a thorough analysis of the origin and characteristics of records series, a knowledge of techniques for the segregation and selection of records, an awareness of the development of research methodologies and needs, and a sequential consideration of administrative, research, and archival values.[49]

Brichford then obliged with a list of records characteristics ranging from age to form to functional elements.

While there is nothing inherently wrong with such an approach, it is only operable if it is done in the context of preappraisal and documentation planning. David Bearman has clearly demonstrated the futility of trying to operate appraisal by examining every record or even every series: the volume and complexity of modern documentation is simply too great.[50] It is evident in certain other kinds of appraisal principles as well. For example, most repositories have adopted a principle along the following lines: *Every archives or manuscript repository may set some date, according to its own peculiar circumstances and history, before which all records discovered are preserved.* Margaret Cross Norton articulated this concept at a very early time.

> A common and helpful device is to set an arbitrary date back of which records are to be considered historical and not subject to destruction....[Why?] There is a pioneer period in every state [Norton is developing this thought from the state government archives perspective] from which comparatively few records have been handed down. Government records are generally not only the most informative on such periods, but often the only records there are. The few records which do not seem to be of much importance take up proportionably little space and can therefore be preserved.[51]

The one caveat I would add to Norton's version of this principle is that the date is not an "arbitrary" one, but it is dependent on careful evaluation and assessment of the institution, subject, or geographic region that the archives serves. Added to this principle might be the fact that this is dependent on the nature of the documentation. Some archivists have shown, for example, that certain kinds of documentation, such as motion picture film, should be kept prior to certain dates because of the scarcity of the documentation.[52] This is an example of how certain conditions of the documentation supersede all basic archival appraisal principles. This kind of understanding cannot be known, however, except through the kind of analysis that is represented in the best archival appraisal work including that of the documentation strategy approach. These dates are, of course, the result of the archivist failing in their appraisal work. It is possible that we may have to move these dates up, especially as the electronic information technology increases and dominates organizations. The documentation strategy approach is one means to prevent this from happening.

Another approach is the use of sampling and reappraisal, two other appraisal approaches generally accepted by American archivists, at least theoretically. Sampling and reappraisal are examples of valid mechanisms to reduce records, already determined to have archival value, in quantity without harming the overall value of these records for researchers. Norton noted many years ago that "practically all government records need weeding to segregate important from ephemeral records."[53] The reason for this is quite clear. Norton noted that the "archivist's dilemma is to decide whether to take the responsibility for destroying historically valuable records embedded in a mass of irrelevant materials or whether somehow to find space for that bulk because it contains valuable data."[54] Statistical and other forms of archival sampling have been developed to assist in reducing the portion of that quantity of documentation that has been shown to have archival value; the enormous bulk of documentation affects not only society, its institutions, but archivists in their ability to manage the documentary heritage for societal welfare. Some, like Karen Benedict, have worried about these kinds of approaches: "When a document is destroyed, it is gone forever." Enduring value suddenly becomes a lesser form of value, continuing value.[55] However, as others like David Bearman have pointed out, such concerns are pointless when the bulk of documentation is so great that not even more than a fraction of it can be examined by archivists.[56] Documentation and other appraisal strategies are one way of determining what portion of documentation should be more closely examined by archivists for appraisal and, ultimately, selection for preservation. Still, we must acknowledge that these are labor-intensive devices that are not the most effective means of documenting our institutions and our society or enabling archival appraisal to be its most effective. And, because of this, a focus on records characteristics will not often help archivists and manuscript curators to determine when to use sampling, and it is this decision that is often the most difficult to make.

A final example concerning a focus on records characteristics and the problems of having such a concentration is the notion of identifying holes in the documental universe. Another archival appraisal principle has emerged, namely that gaps in archival documentation should be identified and possibilities made for filling these gaps by some means. Many archivists are abhorred by the notion that the archivist should do anything more than gather the necessary evidence created by an organization of its activities. But many archivists have pointed to some serious problems about this. Schellenberg, for example, noted that

> while an archivist dealing with modern public records will have great difficulty in reducing them to manageable proportions, he will nevertheless often find that the records he wants were not produced at all....It is a curious anomaly that the more important a matter, the less likely is a complete documentation of it to be found.[57]

In fact, archivists have not examined Schellenberg's comment but have instead rested on some comfort that the examination of the records that exist will document what they need documented and will provide the transactional evidence that is so important to them, as well as the records creators and subsequent users. Oral history is one way that documentary gaps can be filled.

> If the purpose of oral history is to fill gaps in the historical record, this would suggest that the gaps should be defined with care and that the interviewer should formulate with some precision what it is that he is after. If that is not done, oral history could be looked on as little more than an expensive fishing expedition.[58]

The question is how to obtain that precision. Documentation strategies (or other similar macroappraisal approaches) can direct the archivist, working with the oral historian and others such as records creators, to know where and when to ply this trade.

The relatively newly proposed concept of institutional functional analysis, most thoroughly discussed in the aspect of documenting colleges and universities, is another alternative approach to wrestling with the nature of modern institutions. Helen Samuels wrote that

> appraisal decisions must be guided by clearer documentary objectives based on a thorough understanding of the phe-

nomenon or institution to be documented. Since archivists cannot predict future research, the best they can do is to document institutions as adequately as possible. A representative record of the full breadth of an institution is the best insurance that future researchers will be able to answer the questions they choose to ask. Functional analysis makes it possible to select such a record.[59]

There are many similarities with the functional analysis approach and that of the archival documentation strategy. The relevancy of this approach to documenting localities is, of course, that localities are made up of a variety of institutions.

THE DOCUMENTATION OF LOCALITIES AND ARCHIVAL APPRAISAL THEORY AND PRACTICE

The archival or manuscript collection or acquisitions policy is the linchpin of approaches to documenting localities and it is fundamentally based on practical considerations. In other words, the acquisition policy and its use has developed in the vessel of the archival and historical manuscripts repository. Even so, the practical origins of this approach have not made its use consistent nor always very helpful for addressing larger documentary goals (and this is a problem since the crafting of such policies is often carried out for just such purposes). F. Gerald Ham, in his recent basic work on archival appraisal, has criticized the alternative or supplementary approach (depending on your view) being considered in this volume, archival documentation strategies, as "highly theoretical and untested in the crucible of practice." Ham also sees that the need of archivists using documentation strategies to develop a "knowledge of the information universe," mechanism for interinstitutional cooperation, and an "enormous investment in fiscal and human resources required to implement this selection methodology" as all being major obstacles to the use of such strategies.[60]

Ham's questions may appear to be good ones, but a strong case can be made that they are misapplied in his discussion of archival appraisal methodology. It could be asked, for example, what has prevented the more effective use of archival collection policies, if they are so practical? Or, why have the critics of the documentation strategy argued in very opposite ways that the archival documentation strategy has always really been done or that they are inconsistent with archival appraisal theory and principles?[61]

There is, of course, another way of examining such concerns. It is my contention that the lack of a fully developed archival appraisal theory and a lack of knowledge of current appraisal theory and practice has weakened the American archival profession's view, understanding, and appreciation of the archival documentation strategy. These weaknesses will be the focal point for the remainder of this volume. Chapter three will consider some case studies of the use of the archival documentation strategy. Chapter four will describe a process for using the archival documentation strategy in the documenting of localities to demonstrate that it is both practical and necessary in such efforts.

NOTES

1. See his *Modern Archives: Principles and Techniques* (Chicago: University of Chicago Press, 1956), chapter 12.

2. *Archival Theory and Practice in the United States: A Historical Analysis* (Seattle: University of Washington Press, 1983), pp. 6-7.

3. The writings by these individuals and others of this philosophy have been cited at appropriate places throughout this volume.

4. "Managing the Record Rather Than the Relic," *Archives and Manuscripts* 20, no. 1 (1992): 58.

5. "On the Identity of the American Archival Profession: A European Perspective," *American Archivist* 54 (Summer 1991): 399.

6. "Mind over Matter: Towards a New Theory of Archival Appraisal," in *The Archival Imagination: Essays in Honour of Hugh A. Taylor*, ed. Barbara L. Craig (Ottawa: Association of Canadian Archivists, 1992), pp. 40-41.

7. "Archival Practice and the Foundations of Historical Method," *Journal of American History* 78 (June 1991): 234.

8. *The Brown Decades: A Study of the Arts in America 1865-1895* (New York: Dover Publications, 1971; org. pub. 1931), p. 23.

9. *On Doing Local History: Reflections on What Local Historians Do, Why, and What it Means* (Nashville: American Association for State and Local History, 1986), p. 136.

10. "Bostonians and Their Neighbors as Pack Rats," *American Archivist* 24 (April 1961): 157.

11. *Assessing Alabama's Archives: A Plan for the Preservation of the State's Historical Records* (Montgomery: Alabama Historical Records Advisory Board, 1985), pp. 134-35.

12. *The Nature and the Study of History* (Columbus, OH: Charles E. Merrill Books, 1965), p. 4-5.

13. "Oral History," in *New Perspectives on Historical Writing* ed. Peter Burke (University Park: Pennsylvania State University Press, 1991), p. 131.

14. "History At Home," *Minnesota History* 19 (March 1938): 15-17.

15. *History Curatorship* (Washington, DC: Smithsonian Institution Press, 1990), p. 61.

16. "The Archival Edge," *American Archivist* 38 (January 1975): 5-13; "Archival Strategies for the Post-Custodial Era," *American Archivist* 44 (Summer 1981): 207-16; and "Archival Choices: Managing the Historical Record in an Age of Abundance," in *Archival Choices: Managing the Historical Record in an Age of Abundance,* ed. Nancy Peace (Lexington, MA: D.C. Heath, 1984), pp. 11-22.

17. Published as *Archives and Museum Informatics Technical Report,* 3 (Spring 1989) (Pittsburgh, PA: Archives and Museum Informatics).

18. Frank Boles, *Archival Appraisal* (New York: Neal-Schuman, 1991).

19. "Beyond Trivia and Nostalgia: Collaborating in the Construction of a Local History," *International Journal of Oral History* 5, no. 3 (1984): 154-55.

20. "Getting the Most Out of Local History," *Michigan History Magazine* 29 (January-March 1945): 20.

21. *History Curatorship,* p. 67. This volume is a useful introduction to the theoretical and practical means by which museums deal with local history.

22. *Developing Local History Programs in Community Libraries* (Chicago: American Library Association, 1989), p. 23.

23. Robert J. Bailey, "Grassroots History: Collecting and Preserving," *Journal of Mississippi History* 40 (1978): 204-05.

24. This is a viewpoint which I have tried to develop in my *Managing Institutional Archives: Foundational Principles and Practices* (Westport, CT: Greenwood Press, 1992).

25. "Beyond Trivia and Nostalgia," p. 155.

26. "Social Structure and State and Local History," *Western Historical Quarterly* 9 (July 1978): 297-98.

27. "Social Structure," p. 297.

28. *Developing Local History Programs,* p. 7.

29. *Developing Local History Programs*, p. 23.

30. Bailey, "Grass Roots History," p. 214.

31. National Archives and Records Administration, "Records Management Regulations; Final Rules," *Federal Register* 55, no. 127 (July 2, 1990), section 1220.14, p. 27423.

32. "State and Local History, The Bedrock of Our Past," *East Tennessee History Society Publications* 48 (1976): 6.

33. *Independent Historical Societies: An Enquiry Into Their Research and Publication Functions and Their Financial Future* (Boston: Boston Athenaeum, 1962), p. 349.

34. *Independent Historical Societies*, p. 351.

35. See, for example, Charles Phillips and Patricia Hogan, *A Culture at Risk: Who Cares for America's Heritage?* (Nashville: American Association for State and Local History, 1984).

36. Consultative Group on Canadian Archives, *Canadian Archives: Report to the Social Sciences and Humanities Research Council of Canada* (Ottawa: Social Sciences and Humanities Research Council of Canada, 1980), p. 63.

37. Leland Dewitt Baldwin, *The Meaning of America: Essays Toward an Understanding of the American Spirit* (Pittsburgh: University of Pittsburgh Press, 1955), p. 3.

38. James A. Henretta, "The Making of An American Community: A Thirty-Year Retrospective," *Reviews in American History* 16 (September 1988): 506.

39. "Social History and Archival Practice," *American Archivist* 44 (Spring 1981): 113-24.

40. "ACA 1991 Conference Overview," *ACA Bulletin* 15 (July 1991): 25.

41. "Archival Theory Redux and Redeemed: Definition and Context Toward a General Theory," *American Archivist* 54 (Winter 1991): 24.

42. "Developing Collecting Policies for Manuscript Collections," *American Archivist* 47 (Winter 1984): 30-42.

43. *Selecting and Appraising Archives and Manuscripts* (Chicago: Society of American Archivists, 1992), chapter 3.

44. See my *Managing Institutional Archives: Foundational Principles and Practices* (Westport, CT: Greenwood Press, 1992), chapter three for my views on this matter.

45. *Toward A Usable Past: Historical Records in the Empire State* (Albany, NY: New York Historical Records Advisory Board, January 1984), p. 52.

46. See the chapter by William Joyce in *Documenting America: Assessing the Condition of Historical Records in the States* (Albany: Published by the National Association of State Archives and Records Administrators for the National Historical Publications and

Records Commission, 1984). To be fair, it is apparent many programs, in other aspects, are convinced of the need for policies but often do not develop them. In a study of British corporations, for example, it was found that 14 percent had "formal information policies" while 93 percent perceived "information as a resource," needing a policy; see W. J. Martin, C. A. Davies, and A. J. Titterington, "Marketing the Concept of Information Management to Top Executives," *Journal of Information Science* 17, no. 4 (1991): 213.

47. The Historical Society of Western Pennsylvania has issued similar brochures for collecting of materials from the Polish-American, Jewish, and African American communities.

48. Judith E. Endelman, "Looking Backward to Plan for the Future: Collection Analysis for Manuscript Repositories," *American Archivist* 50 (Summer 1987): 348.

49. *Archives & Manuscripts: Appraisal & Accessioning* (Chicago: Society of American Archivists, 1977), p. 2.

50. *Archival Methods*, Archives and Museum Informatics Technical Report, 3 (Spring 1989), chapter two,

51. *Norton on Archives*, pp. 242-43.

52. For example, Sam Kula, *The Archival Appraisal of Moving Images: A RAMP Study with Guidelines* (Paris: UNESCO, 1983).

53. *Norton on Archives*, p. 249.

54. *Norton on Archives*, p. 249.

55. "Invitation to a Bonfire: Reappraisal and Deaccessioning of Records as Collection Management Tools in an Archives—A Reply to Leonard Rapport," *American Archivist* 47 (Winter 1984): 44.

56. *Archival Methods*, Archives and Museum Informatics Technical Report 3 (Spring 1989), chapter one.

57. "Appraisal of Modern Public Records," p. 12.

58. Norman Hoyle, "Oral History," *Library Trends* (July 1972): 67.

59. Helen Willa Samuels, *Varsity Letters: Documenting Modern Colleges and Universities* (Metuchen, NJ: Society of American Archivists and Scarecrow Press, 1992), p. 8.

60. *Selecting and Appraising*, p. 16.

61. See, for example, Terry Abraham, "Collection Policy or Documentation Strategy: Theory and Practice," *American Archivist* 54 (Winter 1991): 44-52.

3

DOCUMENTING LOCALITIES: TWO CASE STUDIES

The purpose of this chapter is to show, in case study form, how the archival documentation strategy can be accomplished in the local setting. The first case study is a hypothetical one, concentrated on the urban environment; this conceptual case study has been enhanced with some real illustrations from Pittsburgh, the present urban environment in which the author operates. The second case study is the result of a preliminary effort to apply practically the documentation strategy to a geographical region.

The initial part of this chapter shows the theoretical utility of the documentation strategy approach. The latter portion shows its limitations, outstanding questions about the approach, and introduces the suggested implementation model described in Chapter 5.

CASE STUDY ONE: ARCHIVISTS AND THE CITY

THE URBAN LANDSCAPE OF ARCHIVAL AND HISTORICAL RE-CORDS REPOSITORIES.

The primary question that the archivist and manuscript curator must always keep in mind is whether society— at least the portion he or she is responsible for—is being adequately documented (although the profession continues to debate the meaning of "adequate"—see Table 3-1) through the careful selection and preservation of eye-readable, visual, audio, audiovisual, and electronic records. No matter how this professional's institutional mission is defined, this question will emerge in some way. A collecting policy restricted to a topical area, such as immigration, will ultimately have to define whether this subject is being adequately documented. A repository with a local mandate will have to reevaluate whether all the nuances and features of local life are being adequately documented. Even an institutional archives will, at some point, have to focus itself on whether it will emphasize not just the internal activities of the organization, but the organization's place in its geographical, social, economic, and other contexts.

This question is, in fact, one that has not only much to do with the mission of the archivist but also the very concept of a historical record. Appraisal, the methodological process— underpinned by both theoretical and practical considerations—that the archivist follows in determining what records should be preserved, has long been a main focal point for the work of this professional. What is ultimately saved determines the nature of much of the archivist's other work and characterizes his or her role in the historical and information professions as one who shapes the documentary heritage.[1] Fundamental to the definition of an archival record is its context, which gives it meaning; this is as crucial as the direct informational content of such records, and, in fact, the informational content is diminished without a full comprehension of this context (see Figure 3-1). The documentation strategy approach is a practical means to deal with and correct such problems.

Apart from the professional context of the appraisal function, appraisal's importance is derived from the notion that a record is not historical or archival until the archivist has determined that the record possesses such value and the record has been removed to an archival facility or the preservation of its informational content secured in some other fashion.[2] The German archival theorist Hans Booms has stated that

Table 3-1. Possible Meanings of "Adequate" Documentation

EVIDENTIAL	All records capturing essential evidence of transactions and activities. Evidence can be defined both in a legalistic sense (introduced in court) or from an administrative and research perspective (valuable for understanding past activities).
INFORMATIONAL	All records possessing value to researchers beyond what an organization or other records-creating entity requires to maintain as evidence. This term has never been precisely defined. Records managers tend not to use it, whereas manuscripts curators tend to use it nearly exclusively. The question worth pondering is whether if all records with evidential value are saved are most informational needs met?
REPRESENTATIVE	Records identified and preserved to capture a documentary accretion that provides selective data about the full range of human and organizational activity, events, trends, and societal groups, ensuring that researchers will have some sense of a particular period or aspect of society.
COMPREHENSIVE	All human and organizational activity, events, trends, and groups are all documented to ensure that future researchers can comprehend a particular period or aspect of society

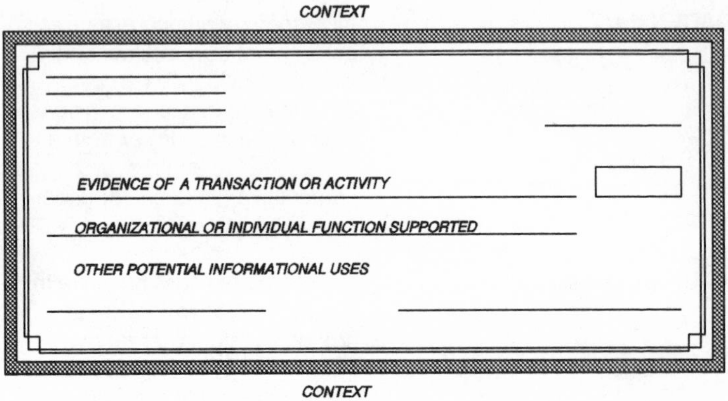

Figure 3-1. Essential Elements of an Archival Record

in appraising the archival value of [the record], and thereby
determining whether it should be preserved permanently in
the archives, the archivist performs the constitutive act by
which societal data are converted into 'historical sources.'
This act...is the archetypal activity of the archivist; it is the
act of forming the documentary heritage—a function that has
been assigned to the archivist by the respective social groups
which he or she serves.[3]

While this view may be a subject of debate by nonarchivists
and some archivists, it is nevertheless true that the chances
of survival of any record outside of an archives facility or the
jurisdiction of an archival program (archival records can be
maintained in offices of creation provided they are governed
by appropriate policy) are considerably reduced. Such a
matter takes on significance in considering the documenting
of localities, since such documentation can take place only
through cooperative ventures that stress both collecting and
the establishing of new and viable institutional archives.

It is an understatement, therefore, that historians, historic preservationists, genealogists, social scientists, and
other researchers should be interested in the archival ap-

praisal process. That the historian has been so interested can be seen in a number of ways, ranging from influencing the creation of new kinds of historical manuscript and archival programs to aiding existing archives and historical records programs in the acquisition of important collections of historical sources. The creation of college and university archives and special collections operations has often occurred because of the interests and research needs of historians.[4] Just as importantly, the changing research practices and interests of historians have led archivists to reevaluate and, sometimes, refocus their appraisal and acquisition practices, a relationship most clearly seen in the last twenty-five years in the realm of social and women's history.[5] More recent calls for resolving the crisis in the public status of historical research and writing has led to pleas for a new kind of community history in which the historian is part of the community and does research more relevant to the community than to academic colleagues;[6] this approach is very similar to the archival documentation strategy method. There is ample evidence of a symbiotic relationship between archivists and their researchers; interest in use and actual use, subject knowledge, research experience, and other qualities brought to archives by research patrons should be of utility to archivists as they consider all aspects of their work.

Despite such concerns and interests, however, archivists and historians have nevertheless long operated from the assumption that society will be adequately documented as a natural result of creating and sustaining historical records collecting agencies and institutional archives. The attitude displayed has been almost a laissez-faire approach to appraisal and documentation. Archivists have tended to view the issue of documenting society as one that would be achieved as a result of archival programs' developing and carrying out their institutional acquisitions policies. Historians have generally operated with the assumption that the majority of records necessary for their research would be there in the repositories when they went looking for them. Both historians and archivists have seemed to suggest that adding together all the historical and archival records held in archival and historical records repositories would result in a broad enough, if not thorough, documentation of the past. Historians' discoveries, from time to time, of different ways of looking at the past—such as the initial interest in the history of the city spurred by Arthur M. Schlesinger, Sr. and the enthusiastic flourishing of the "new" urban history of the late 1960s and early 1970s—have generally led historians either to use existing sources in new ways or for them to encourage appropriate institutions to collect additional sources. Archivists have generally been responsive to such interests by historians and other of their researchers, although the matter of whether true partnerships and cooperative ventures have developed is debatable once a few noteworthy examples, such as the continuing work of the American Institute of Physics and the Women's History Sources project of the 1970s, are discussed.

Has the American city been adequately documented because of the work of archivists and the interests of historians and other researchers using urban archival sources? Without question, there are considerable holdings of archival and historical records with important information relating to the cities (see Figure 3-2). Yet, it is relatively easy to identify major gaps in virtually any aspect of urban life and experience, some of which by themselves indicate that the documentation is flawed. The archival records of municipal government, sources that are essential not only to understanding the governance of the city but many other aspects as well, are given haphazard care throughout the United States. Local government archives are underdeveloped and are in existence in only a portion of the cities.[7] Cultural organizations (such as public libraries and museums), essential to the life of the urban areas, have also not been adequately documented. Public library archives are virtually nonexistent, and work in establishing archival programs in museums, arts organizations, and other such entities has only seriously begun over the past decade.[8] While portions of the documentary record of these aspects of urban life are available for research, it should be obvious that historians and other researchers must work to discover what they need

Figure 3-2. Selected General Strengths and Weaknesses in Urban Documentation

and, more importantly, there has been little thought given as to how these areas should be documented.

There is, of course, a significant degree of irony in considering the documentation of the city, since the interest in the preservation of such resources has been evident for a very long time. First, historical records repositories, such as historical societies, have always tended to cluster in urban areas because of the existence of educated urban elites—often defensively reacting to the more dramatic and noticeable societal changes—and large educational and cultural institutions. These repositories have often collected the historical records of individuals, families, businesses, organizations, and governments located nearby, both because of the obvious convenience as well as purposeful efforts to document the elites associated with these cultural institutions. Second, although institutional archives represent a too small portion of all the archival repositories in this country, they have often been established in larger corporations and organizations and these have also been more prone to concentrate in or— as suburbanization and, later, industrial parks developed— near urban areas. Despite problems of access to these records, the creation of such repositories has provided additional opportunities for urban historical research. Third, professional historians have been interested in urban history for well over half a century, and the richness and intensity of their interest has been well reflected in their numerous writings about this topic. Additionally, the amateurs and antiquarians of the previous century also drew attention to the importance of the history of cities and the urban records, leading to the placement of many important collections in urban historical societies and libraries. Fourth, and finally, some of the most advanced communication systems—potential candidates for archival documentation—were born and developed in the cities. William Ellery Channing's 1855 address to the Smithsonian Institution about the telegraph noted that the telegraph's

> function is not to connect distant towns or independent centres of life and activity with each other, but it is to organize a single city or town so as to bring every subordinate part into relation with its centre of government and direction. Its purpose is to multiply points of communication, to cover the surface of the municipal body as thickly...with telegraphic signalizing points as the surface of the human body is covered with nervous extremities or papillae, the whole being intelligently connected into a system by which the municipal body shall understand itself in every part, and shall have a common life and vital functions for its own essential purposes.[9]

Yet, a half century later, people are still trying to figure out *whether* archivists and historians can *hope* to document an organism that was partially possible because of increasingly sophisticated means of communication, the establishment of government, and the sustenance of commercial and cultural organizations.

Assumptions about the documentation of cities have been, of course, considerably shaken in the last generation, especially during the past decade. For one, it is obvious that, left to chance, significant aspects of urban life might not be documented, or, at the least, that important sources will not be adequately preserved. A glance at the types of archival and manuscript repositories that have been established in ten of the most populous cities in this country suggests this problem (see Figure 3-3). Except for Philadelphia, there are

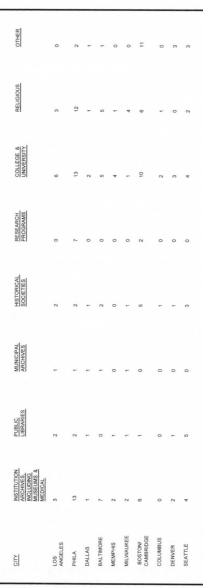

CITY	INSTITUTION ARCHIVES, INCLUDING MUSEUMS & MEDICAL	PUBLIC LIBRARIES	MUNICIPAL ARCHIVES	HISTORICAL SOCIETIES	RESEARCH PROGRAMS	COLLEGE & UNIVERSITY	RELIGIOUS	OTHER
LOS ANGELES	3	2	1	2	0	6	3	0
PHILA	13	2	1	2	7	13	12	2
DALLAS	1	1	1	1	0	2	1	1
BALTIMORE	7	0	1	2	0	5	5	1
MEMPHIS	2	1	0	0	0	4	1	0
MILWAUKEE	2	1	1	1	0	1	4	0
BOSTON/ CAMBRIDGE	6	1	0	5	2	10	6	11
COLUMBUS	0	0	0	1	0	2	1	0
DENVER	2	1	0	1	0	3	0	3
SEATTLE	4	5	0	3	0	4	2	3

Figure 3-3. Archival and Historical Records Repositories by Type in Major Urban Areas (*Source: Directory of Archives and Manuscript Repositories in the United States, 2nd ed. Phoenix, AZ: Oryx Press for the NHPRC, 1988*).

few if any institutional archives; the records of major corporations and organizations seem to be in jeopardy. Only five
of the ten cities have any semblance of a municipal government records program; while local government records tend
to show up in public libraries and historical societies, these
arrangements usually guarantee the preservation of only a
portion of the government archival records. Few medical and
health institutions have made any commitment to establishing institutional archives. While there are a large variety
of archival and historical records repositories in the cities,
the burden for documenting the cities seems to have fallen
on colleges and universities, local historical societies, and
museums.

The nature of this haphazard organization of archival and
manuscript repositories can be clearly seen by a closer
examination of the archival community in Pittsburgh. The
oldest repository is that of the Historical Society of Western
Pennsylvania, founded in 1879, and possessing a broad
mandate to document the Western Pennsylvania region. This
institution has tended to focus on the papers of prominent
individuals and families, although since the late 1980s it has
broadened its mission to one more dictated by a social
history agenda with broad representation in its collections
of ethnic groups and minorities. The University of Pittsburgh
has gained a position since the mid-twentieth century as the
next major repository with an interest in documenting Pittsburgh and its hinterlands. The Archives of Industrial Society,
established in 1963 to focus on the documentation of the
region's industrial society and housed at the university, was
a conscious effort to deal with the omissions in the acquisition policy of the Historical Society and to support the
research needs and interests of the urban and social historians located at the University of Pittsburgh and other
institutions of higher education.

Beyond these two major repositories, a broad range of
archival and historical manuscripts repositories has developed. These include special focused collecting programs
such as the Archives of Scientific Philosophy in the Twentieth Century at the University of Pittsburgh (an important
topic of research and teaching at the university), the Fred

Rogers Archives at the University of Pittsburgh School of Library and Information Science, the Hunt Institute for Botanical Documentation at Carnegie Mellon University, and institutional archives such as those of Duquesne University, Carnegie Mellon University, the Pittsburgh Theological Seminary, the Episcopal and Catholic Dioceses of Pittsburgh, the Sisters of Mercy of Pittsburgh, and Allegheny County, and a host of other smaller institutional programs. All of these other programs are creations of the past two or three decades and remain relatively small in staff and resources, and, as a result, seriously limited in their effectiveness. Furthermore, they reveal an extremely haphazard approach to the documentation of Pittsburgh and its vicinity. There are obvious gaps: Where are the archives of large businesses and social and cultural organizations? Why does the main county government possess a program while the City of Pittsburgh and other smaller town and city governments have no archives and records management programs? There are also conflicting missions: the Historical Society of Western Pennsylvania has developed a collecting policy as if these other programs were nonexistent. The development of more specialized collecting programs has proceeded as if the other major repositories were not operating. Such documentary confusion in Pittsburgh is typical of other urban areas in the United States.

The general lack of *systematic* cooperation among such institutions and these institutions' limited resources for acquiring and preserving archival records and historical manuscripts additionally weakens any confidence in the thorough documentation of urban life, except through chance. The chancy aspect of present adequate urban documentation can be seen in the Philadelphia "model" of private historical society, municipal government archives, and urban (social history) archives at a university that resulted from "sharply differing circumstances: an early-nineteenth-century combination of antiquarianism and local patriotism in the case of the Historical Society; civic reform, certainly rare in Philadelphia, in the case of the City Archives; and collegiate prosperity, now even rarer than reform, together with the ghetto unrest of the late sixties, in the case of the

Urban Archives." As Fredric Miller, the author of this analysis has noted, there really is "no blueprint [for other cities] to follow."[10] Except, it almost appears as if a city like Pittsburgh followed the blueprint, since the configuration of repositories is virtually identical.

The problem with the lack of cooperation is evident in the fact that the potential quantity of records that archivists could examine is so great that they can only look at a very minor portion. One archivist has suggested that "there can be little doubt that hundreds of times the volume of twentieth century records ever offered to archives are stowed in closets, basements and storage rooms."[11] The sight of archivists and manuscript curators either competing or refusing to work with each other is a ridiculous predicament to have given the immensity of the task in documenting society. This is probably partly why Sam Bass Warner at the 1971 Society of American Archivists meeting called for the creation of "a few well-managed and well-funded specialized [urban] archives." Warner stated,

> We are the most prolific record-producing society in the history of mankind, and a mere call for putting more of these records in order is an irresponsible social act. As I see it even if all the public records of our urban governments were organized into well-selected and well-managed archives I can't think urban history would improve markedly.[12]

It is as if Warner had been describing the present situation in Pittsburgh. On one hand, there has been a coalescence of individuals interested in protecting the records, historic sites, architectural landmarks, and other aspects of Pittsburgh, formed in the 1980s into a citizens' watchdog group known as the Committee on Pittsburgh Archaeology and History. This Committee maintained pressure on Allegheny County, for example, to establish an archives and records management program, certainly one important factor why this county government finally established a bona fide program of this sort in mid-1990. But beyond such cooperation, and the informal gathering of archivists, rare books, and special collections staffs monthly (in a group called the Curators' Coalition), there is little evidence of systematic planning for cooperative ventures in Pittsburgh. At one point, in the late 1980s, the Carnegie Institution, Carnegie-Mellon University, and the University of Pittsburgh discussed ideas for renovating and jointly administering a facility for the storage and use of archives, historical manuscripts, and rare books; the venture ended because details about each institution's fair share could not be resolved. Another effort, working through the Pittsburgh Regional Library Consortium, examined the possibility of placing a regional conservation center in the new facilities of the Historical Society of Western Pennsylvania planned for a 1996 opening; again these efforts broke apart because of questions of costs, ownership and governance, and related cooperative issues. As a result, cooperation in Pittsburgh has been throttled at all points. Basic collecting and acquisition is done in isolation, as if each repository were fully responsible for documenting all of the urban area. Institutional archives are established and develop, virtually ignored by their collecting counterparts as important elements of the archival community, at least in the complete documentation of Pittsburgh.

It is also true, despite some of the problems already mentioned, that the urban area offers a greater accumulation of documentation than other geographical areas. Two urban archaeologists noted, for example, that

> the urban archaeological resource presents opportunities to formulate and test hypotheses about human behavior in a variety of behavioral contexts and to combine several independent sets of data in broadly-based research strategies. In addition to the archaeological collections, there is a wealth of preserved documents (newspapers, magazines, city directories, deed and title records, census reports, church records, and insurance maps, to name a few) and a fair number of surviving participants.[13]

It is, of course, partly the wealth of the surviving documentation that has attracted historians to the city, promising new ways that the past could be researched, reconstructed, and understood. It is also why the urban area remains an excellent arena in which to develop and experiment with new

ways of purposeful selection— such as the archival documentation strategy concept—from the vast quantities of
recorded information in order to shape an appropriate documentary heritage that allows questions about the urban past
to be asked and answered. Cities like Pittsburgh are literally
awash in documentation, ranging from the old steel industry
to the newly emerging high-tech industry and from large
institutions of higher education to numerous cultural organizations and civic groups, all benefiting an older city
dating from the eighteenth century. The documentation
strategy offers some hope for rectifying some of the inade-
quacies of urban documentation that I have discussed thus
far, aiding both the archivist in managing the documentary
heritage and the historian who needs access to as complete
documentation as is possible.

THE ARCHIVAL DOCUMENTATION STRATEGY AS A MECHANISM FOR DOCUMENTING THE CITY

Archival documentation strategies are important for consideration by the archival and historical (and museum and
related) professions because they provide a way of dealing
with the inadequacy of resources possessed by these professions and their institutions to cope with all the information
possessing historical value. There is, simply put, too much
information found in textual, artifactual, audio, digital, and
other information sources for archivists and historians to
examine, appraise, select, preserve, and interpret all of it.
The documentation strategy concept provides one promising
means to address such challenges in a logical and informed
manner.[14]

The archival documentation strategy has been defined in
Chapter 2 of this volume. This strategy is, as has been
suggested already, a relatively new archival concept, one that
emerged in the mid-1980s because of frustrations by archivists in coping with the vastness and increasing complexity
of the documentation. The origins of the concept can be
discerned in its most salient attributes, which are its analytical nature, planned response, cooperative approach, and
stress on ongoing issues and activities or geographical areas.

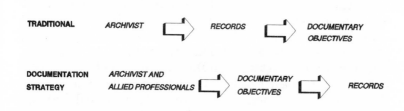

Figure 3-4. The Analytical Strength of the Archival Documentation Strategy

The analytical nature of the documentation strategy is its focus on a thorough definition of documentation needs before any actual records have been examined (see Figure 3-4). What is desired to be known, according to present knowledge and conceptions of future research (about as best as can be determined), about a particular topic or geographic area is ascertained and the existing documentation evaluated to determine not only what should be saved but what gaps there are and how they can be supplemented. The focus is on the importance of an ongoing activity or in identifying the important features of a geographical region rather than their informational byproducts. This approach represents a departure from traditional archival appraisal practice which has been records-centered. Archival approaches to selecting records have all generally started with the examination of the records themselves and discerning whether the records have intrinsic, informational, evidential, or other such values that merit preservation. Even efforts to "document" a broad topical area have relied upon techniques such as records surveying that identifies only existing documentation and then determines how the topic will be documented with these sources. The traditional archival approach can be seen in that some archivists have confused documentation strategies with other approaches such as surveying, field work and collecting, and the process of developing institutional collection policies.[15]

The planned aspect of the archival documentation strategy is another of its salient features. The documentation strategy process directs archivists and their colleagues to think about what the *ideal* documentation of a particular topic or region *should* look like. In one regional test of the documentation strategy, archivists and historians were asked to define their scope or sphere of activity, determine the main characteristics of the region's historical development, evaluate and compare the existing documentation quality and significance of each of these characteristics, prioritize documentation activities, and conclude with a statement of the *desired* archival documentation for the locality. This test constitutes the second part of this chapter. This process is also intended to identify the necessary roles of various archival repositories and other institutions. This is, as well, a departure from traditional archival appraisal practice which has been often merely responses to offered donations, threatened destruction of valuable records, or the changing interests of researchers. F. Gerald Ham's 1974 presidential address to the Society of American Archivists, and a seminal writing in the ultimate articulation of the documentation strategy approach, lamented that archivists had become reactive custodians and that their holdings had been transfixed by this approach. While it is important that archivists pay attention to changing research trends, Ham suggested, he also noted a "dilemma."

> Most researchers are caught in their own concerns and do not worry about all the history that needs to be written; yet in terms of documentary preservation this is precisely what the archivist must do. Small wonder, then, that archival holdings too often reflected narrow research interests rather than the broad spectrum of human experience.[16]

The archival documentation strategy is designed specifically to overcome these and other problems. Archivists and colleagues work through a well-defined series of steps that evaluate a topic or region, determine documentation priorities, assess existing documentation strengths and weaknesses, and plan actions to acquire adequate documentation, all of this reflected in a written plan.

The documentation strategy is also a cooperative venture involving records creators, custodians, and users. Although archival cooperation has been an issue long discussed in the archival profession and its literature, this cooperation has tended to be restricted by archivists to other archivists and between archival repositories in areas such as national descriptive systems and regional collecting networks. I have already alluded to the fact that these cooperative ventures have not worked as well as planned. The documentation strategy points to a different cooperative issue—the need for archivists to work with other records custodians, creators, and users because of the interrelated nature of modern documentation. This documentary relationship attests to the fact that few activities or institutions are not continuously affected by external influences such as regulations, law, competitors, political events and trends, and so forth. Records managers often note, for example, that seventy or more percent of an institution's records are form determined; what is also revealing is that the content of many of these forms are determined by external governmental, fiscal, legal, and other requirements. The value of the documentation strategy for fostering cooperation has been pointed to by a number of appraisal archivists as possessing great value. In a recent review of changing archival appraisal approaches, Margaret Hedstrom stated that

> documentation strategies offer a new approach to understanding the broad context for specific appraisal decisions. The concept is based on a recognition that records are interrelated, just as the processes that create then are interrelated. Therefore, custodians and creators of records from many institutions need to be involved in defining a documentation strategy in order to illuminate the general terrain of documentation on a subject, functional area, or region.[17]

Finally, the documentation strategy approach is concentrated on an ongoing or active issue or a geographical area. It is not fixed on past events and their documentary remains, an approach that has generally governed the work of archivists and manuscript curators in collecting repositories. Archivists are often called in to examine potential archival records that have substantial age and specific occasions associated with them; even institutional archivists are sometimes removed from the management of their organization's current records in a way that minimizes their ability to make appraisal decisions that possess the appropriate timeliness. Problems such as these sometime lead archivists to resort to simplistic lists of records type that only roughly approximate the documentation that is desired.[18] The documentation strategy is intended to assist archivists to identify and preserve documentation of *ongoing* activities which may be risky in terms of selecting what activities might seem important for present and future researchers, but which is absolutely essential for safeguarding documentation that is appearing in fragile electronic and other forms that require early intervention by archivists and, in some cases, a literal restructuring of the records. This approach has struck some archivists as heretical to accepted archival practices, but it is very likely that many basic archival practices will be transformed (and at the least modified) by new information technologies.[19]

What are, then, the implications of the archival documentation strategy for urban history and urban historians and other researchers? The primary implication is that the documentation strategy can provide a mechanism that has the potential for enabling a more informed determination of what urban records should be preserved. This determination includes provision for encouraging institutional records creators to establish or support better archival programs that may make the ultimate difference in whether these records are saved or not. Existing archival and historical manuscripts repositories cannot handle in a satisfactory manner the universe of archival documentation (see Figure 3-5). The documentation strategy strengthens the selection process. This latter function is also at the heart of the secondary implication of the strategy for urban history and historians— it creates a mechanism by which urban historians can more actively participate with archivists and other disciplines in shaping the urban documentary record. Both of these implications are worth some further discussion.

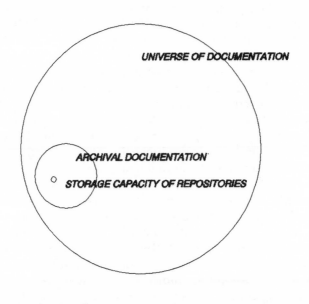

Figure 3-5. The Challenge of Archival and Historical Manuscripts Repositories in the Documentary Universe

THE ADVANTAGES OF MULTIDISCIPLINARY APPROACHES TO DOCUMENTING URBAN LIFE

Archivists have sometimes tended to be a rather insulated lot, although certainly no more or less than any other professional group, with a perspective that is confined largely to their own institutional and professional parameters. This might be viewed as contrary to a field that has declared itself to possess a multidisciplinary foundation, primarily articulated in statements and assessments of their graduate and continuing education programs.[20] But this multidisciplinary base is not an interdisciplinary one; that is, archivists might state their desire to have a broad range of knowledge, but they have not necessarily decided that they must always use this knowledge or, and more importantly, cooperate with other disciplines to accomplish their basic mission. Like so many other professionals, archivists have generally viewed themselves as essentially self-reliant, writing their own code of ethics, developing their own standards, and certifying their own practitioners.

It is evident that archivists now view their role as a selector of recorded information that leads to a documentation of society based on fundamental principles of archival appraisal; this view is a result of the archivist's recognition of the immense volume of records, the interrelatedness of records (even those produced by diverse institutions and organizations), and the increasing diversity of recorded information forms.[21] But two problems persist here. First, the archivist relies on archival approaches to select, although these principles have been increasingly shaped or influenced by library collection development, historiographical trends, and other fields. Second, the archivist has restricted his or her activity to the traditional documentary forms, such as letters, memoranda, minutes, statistical reports, and the like—whether in paper or electronic media. Information valuable or essential to understanding any topic, geographic area, event, movement, individual's life, a family's development, or society can be found in a tremendous number of "sources" (see Figure 3-6). Artifacts, archaeological remains, popular culture, oral tradition, folklore, publications, movies and television, and archives and manuscripts can all play important roles in, first, documenting society, and, second, understanding society. If the archivist is truly interested in documenting society, then he or she must consider these other information sources and the approaches of other disciplines in selecting and preserving them.

Consider just one source that supplements, or adds to, in important ways, traditional archival sources. In John Fiske's provocative writings on popular culture, he has noted that the "people make popular culture at the interface between everyday life and the consumption of the products of the cultural industries." Or, "popular culture is made by various formations of subordinated or disempowered people out of the resources, both discursive and material, that are provided by the social system that disempowers them."[22] The

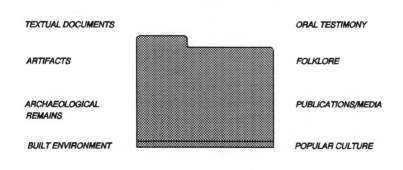

TEXTUAL DOCUMENTS

ARTIFACTS

ARCHAEOLOGICAL
REMAINS

BUILT ENVIRONMENT

ORAL TESTIMONY

FOLKLORE

PUBLICATIONS/MEDIA

POPULAR CULTURE

Figure 3-6. The Variety of Sources for Documenting Any Aspect of Society

results of these interfaces are texts that outsiders can use to interpret the people's activities and lifestyles and that the people themselves use to give meaning to their own existence. These texts are far different from traditional archival sources. For John Fiske, then, a text is a beach, a mall, or the image of the popular singer-actress Madonna. Or, as George Lipsitz has found, television, music, film, and literature have become a significant source of providing a collective memory for people that structure their lives and help to provide them a sense of meaning. Lipsitz noted that "historical memories and historical evidence can no longer be found solely in archives and libraries; they pervade popular culture and public discourse as well."[23] The questions that must be asked are whether the archivist can document society with such a restricted view of informational sources, and, just as importantly, whether the archivist plays (or should play) a role in selecting informational sources beyond the traditional documentary ones.

The need to document urban areas in a planned manner that brings together a wide variety of disciplines and their variant perspectives and approaches can also be discerned by noting the same breadth of research approaches to urban life. Two commentators stated it this way:

> The traditional disciplines through which we approach the city as an object of historical study have had to make room for the city as a subtopic of increasing importance—city literature or city painting, urban psychology or sociology, and history of the city. In the past few decades a new multidisciplinary field, urban studies, has attempted to integrate this knowledge. But in its complexity the city remains resistant to scholarly synthesis, and our working definitions of it remain largely determined by the individual disciplines.[24]

There are, of course, also precedents for the interdisciplinary documentation of urban areas in historical research. The Philadelphia Social History Project (PSHP), as just one example, sought-not altogether successfully—to examine how a wide variety of historical variables—markets, immigration, industry, politics, population composition and distribution, transportation, occupational structure, families, and wealth— affected opportunities in the city. To gather relevant information about individuals and these variables, the PSHP used a variety of source material including abolition organization and Quaker manuscript censuses, federal population manuscript schedules, federal manufacturing manuscript census schedules, and published business directories. It is not difficult to expand these sources to a far greater variety of archival and artifactual materials. As Theodore Hershberg noted, the "study of complex historical processes such as urbanization and industrialization require first, an interdisciplinary research effort, and second, the concentration of resources."[25] In a less structured way, such research has also been carried out in other cities like Pittsburgh in which clusters of urban historians and their graduate students have gathered.[26] Such concerns obviously demonstrate the need for archivists and others, striving to document the city and understand its past, to bring together a variety of disciplines concerned with urban history and life.

Over the past decade or more there has appeared a growing quantity of urban comparative studies that examine cities in a variety of national settings, taking issues of concern to urbanists and determining how these issues are affected by different political, social, and cultural contexts.[27] These comparative studies, along with the rise of quantitative history over the past two decades, have certainly caused archivists, as just one example, to rethink how they treated a portion of their holdings, including how they described such materials and what they sought to collect. Manuscript collections supposedly documenting elites were reexamined for what they revealed about social mobility, family change and life, and other aspects of urban existence. As Conzen has written, the

> principal methodological innovations of the new urban history involved techniques for using systematic sources of individual-level data such as manuscript censuses, city directories, tax assessment lists, credit rating reports, and vital records to compile a set of common variables that could readily be linked to one another, coded, aggregated, and statistically correlated with the aid of standard computer software packages.[28]

What this suggests is, of course, the value of the researcher, historians, and others, assisting the archivist to ensure that the right sources are preserved in the first place.

Sociologists, anthropologists, and others, while perhaps complicating the logistics of the appraisal or documentation process, are also vital to ensuring that adequate documentation of urban life is acquired. The view of the sociologist, transfixed on such issues as city growth and patterns of growth—including suburbanization—and other matters such as settlement and "nonmetropolitan turnaround," has of course affected historical question-asking and answer-seeking.[29] It is not difficult to see how a sociologist, participating in an urban documentation effort, could assist basic definitions of geographical scope, topical definitions, and broad models of interpretation that would lead to more useful archival appraisal, selection, and documentation. Anthropologists have also made the study of the urban setting a major focus of their work. At first urban anthropology, emerging seriously in the 1960s, was focused on urban poverty and ethnicity, largely stimulated by the unrest in the

cities, decline of population and resulting economic stagna-
tion, and the social programs of the federal administrations.
Anthropologists studied the "tribes" in the cities, just as they
studied cultures in Pacific Islands and African wildernesses.
More recently, however, anthropologists have made an effort
to expand their research, examining relations between various population groups, the processes of the city such as
political governance with these groups and community and
neighborhood structures, and the like. These new interests
have led to modification of methodologies and such research
is now characterized by interdisciplinary teams of researchers using surveys, examination of documents, inter-
viewing, and other approaches that require the use of a
varied information sources.[30] Bringing together a multiplicity of disciplines has many benefits. Writing about urban
folklore, for example, Martin Laba stated that the

> discipline of folklore has yet to develop a theoretical perspec-
> tive which is consonant with urban experience. Folklorists
> have failed to apprehend the city as a whole, and continue to
> dissect the urban environment into ethnic or generic com-
> partments for the examination of items of folklore trans-
> planted from rural to urban settings.[31]

The structure of bringing together numerous disciplines
offers the possibility that the folklorist would expand his or
her vision, and the archivist committed to documenting
urban life and society would welcome the perspective and
advice of the folklorist. While the archivist might believe he
or she has documented an aspect of urban life, the folklorist
opens up a new vista for understanding the value of other
sources of nontraditional archival materials and the limitations of the archival materials.

The importance of having multidisciplinary documentation efforts can also be seen by the manner in which archives
gather their material and the gaps in the materials that they
collect. In writing about folklore archives, this telling statement was made.

> Because folklore archives in the United States...are not oper-
> ating with sizeable budgets, they become depositories for
> collections rather than research facilities. Accordingly, they
> depend on nonprofessional collectors, often students in col-

lege or university folklore classes, for their materials although professional folklorists have made contributions as well. The strength of this system of recording folk traditions is that nonprofessionals often have entree to situations unknown to professionals; the weakness is that collected records are less complete and less accurate than they might be.[32]

This is a familiar lament, one sounded by many kinds of cultural organizations other than just archives. The potential meaning of material culture and the importance and difficulty of its selection for preservation can be seen in how a museum seeks to use material culture remains (and, of course, other more traditional textual sources) to interpret the past for the public. An excellent glimpse into this process is seen in the Historical Society of Pennsylvania's recent exhibition, "Finding Philadelphia's Past," and a series of essays published in the Society's journal about the production of this exhibition. The exhibition sought not only to provide interpretation about the history of Philadelphia but to provide understanding about the role of collecting artifacts and archives by institutions such as historical societies. The exhibition showed that one institution cannot gather all the important relics and information sources of the past and that items collected for one purpose often take on different meanings as time passes. The symbol of the exhibition became Benjamin Franklin's bifocals.[33] In the same fashion, the archivist must keep in mind, in his or her quest to document society, all of the variety of sources that might not be in their archives and the meaning of the archival sources that they do hold. While perhaps the archivist would not relish the symbol of Franklin's bifocals, it is still important that he or she develop the widest possible perspective and most energetic, proactive stance when it comes to archival appraisal and the documentation of society.

APPLYING THE DOCUMENTATION STRATEGY TO URBAN LIFE: OTHER CASE STUDIES

In concluding the first section of this chapter, it would be worthwhile to describe briefly several case studies of the use of documentation strategies in urban areas. All of these are efforts to provide improved documentation of areas of activity in urban settings that have either been neglected or that have proved to be difficult to manage. These case studies should also reflect the ample opportunities there are for historians and others to participate in or promote urban documentation strategies.

The first case study is a hypothetical one, but it is valuable to consider because it reveals the full potential of the documentation strategy approach. Philip N. Alexander and Helen W. Samuels have written an essay on documenting the high-technology companies that ring Boston on Route 128 and that are the direct result of features of the Boston area such as its universities, government, and other businesses. It is the interrelatedness of the universities, government at all levels, businesses, and the city itself that has spawned the high-technology companies but this interrelatedness has also worked against the adequate documentation of these companies. There are virtually no archives, institutional or collecting, involved in seeking to document the high-technology work of these companies. The reasons for this are clear. Scientific research is characterized by elaborate team efforts cutting across company and university and by complicated combinations of federal and private funding, while efforts to commercialize the products of such research may be seen more traditionally as the province of one company. This situation has left the issue of how to document a post-WWII phenomenon that is extremely complex, but nevertheless essential for understanding both Boston and modern science and technology. This is not an area that can be adequately managed by traditional collecting or through standard archival approaches.

Samuels and Alexander have carefully suggested how this can be accomplished, starting with a set of key questions in technical, economic, social, political, and educational functions. After this, there needs to be consideration of major objectives, revealing what we have been considering in this book:

> A major objective is to target particular firms, products, events, and individuals to be documented. The strategy assumes that not everything can or should be documented. A selection process is developed that will adequately document

the successes, failures, anomalies, and routine events encompassing the Route 128 phenomenon. Though the advisors may start with impressionistic feelings...the actual selection should be based on solid background research and structured guidelines. If necessary, additional expertise should be enlisted to help address specific areas in greater detail. Historians, economists, sociologists, company administrators, and government officials may be canvassed for their special experience and understanding of the possible focus of a documentation strategy.[34]

After this, a process can be followed that includes an analysis of the nature and quality of the documentation of Route 128, a plan for ensuring the preservation and availability of the documentation, and a mechanism for continuing and refining the work as necessary.

Other efforts to apply the archival documentation strategy to the urban setting are also beginning to emerge. The first of these is an ambitious effort to develop over two years a full documentation plan for the city of Milwaukee. Supported by funds from the National Historical Publications and Records Commission (NHPRC), this project started in mid-1989 and was completed in 1992. Its main aim was to bring together representatives of archival repositories and related institutions (such as the public library and municipal history museum) to determine how effectively Milwaukee has been documented through its ad-hoc approach (the creation and functioning of collecting programs)[35] and what would need to be done to correct problems and fill in documentary gaps. The project focused its attention on assisting the existing repositories to create adequate descriptions of their holdings so that a multi-institutional collection analysis project could be carried out that identifies both strengths and weaknesses in Milwaukee's documentation, allowing for future documentation planning to be done.[36] Although it is too soon to evaluate the final implications of this project, especially since what has been done is only a preliminary analysis phase to help determine priorities for documentation strategy initiatives, reports have been positive that the Milwaukee archival and historical community is working together for common objectives better than it has anytime in the past. The multi-

institutional focus of the documentation strategy, even apart
from its final products and successes, seems to be a powerful
mechanism by which to bring together archival custodians
and users.

Another urban application of the documentation strategy
was the efforts of the District of Columbia's Historical Records Advisory Board (DCHRAB) to determine how the strategy (again with the benefit of NHPRC funding, albeit very
modest) can be used to gain adequate documentation of the
numerous regional governmental and quasigovernmental
authorities in the Washington metropolitan area. Not only
are these authorities important for the governance and
quality of life of the District, but they have created records
that are important for understanding many aspects of daily
living in this city, including transportation, parks and recreation, urban planning, utilities, and other basic services.
Many of the records of these authorities have been either lost
or poorly maintained—with no provision for researchers.
This two-year project was an endeavor to use the documentation strategy approach to unite representatives of these
authorities with archivists and historians and to determine
priorities for collecting and the establishment of institutional
archives programs. Like Milwaukee, final analysis is impossible, but the District efforts have also brought together
groups and institutions for the first time that had had little
contact with each other. This project, at the least, developed
some basic issues and topics that are crucial to the authorities and that, in some cases, provide unique sources of
historical information for researchers. Whether the project
leads to resolution of how to document fully the importance
of these authorities in the life of the District's residents or
not remains to be seen, but the documentation strategy as
a mechanism for enabling this to occur appears to be
excellent.

Not all documentation strategies have to be dependent on
external funds or have a broad scope. The archival agency
of the Archdiocese of Chicago, as another urban example,
has made a recent effort to use the documentation strategy
concept in documenting Catholicism in that city. Before the
application of the strategy, it was felt that the acquisition of

archival material had been too informal, resulting in a "collection somewhat top heavy with the papers of the movers and shakers of the Archdiocese—and only the ordained movers and shakers at that. There were vast areas of concern where Catholicism had both flourished and languished in the Archdiocese which remained not only neglected, but ignored."[37] The archivists of the Diocese developed a list of Catholic institutions and a list of main activities (education, pastoral service, human service, social and political concerns, and curial affairs) and then proceeded to examine the existing documentation related to these broad areas of activities that captured the essence of Chicago Catholicism. The result was an agenda for renewed acquisition by the Diocesan archives and other repositories within the Chicago area that might acquire historical records related to Catholicism.

As a final example, we could consider what should be going on in the Pittsburgh area. As our earlier references to this geographic area suggested, each repository seems to be conducting its work as if it is a solitary player on the documentary landscape. What cooperation exists is very informal, more in the nature of referring researchers to other repositories, rather than anything nearly as ambitious as cooperative appraisal, collecting, and documentation efforts. At the Historical Society of Western Pennsylvania, discussions about collecting are guided more by a knowledge of the diversity and richness of the history of this city rather than by any realization that there are other collecting repositories or institutional archives with legitimate stakes in this. What could be occurring is quite simple in conception, although it would require expenditures of resources (primarily staff time) in planning *before* implementation (see Table 3-2). First, representatives of archival and historical records repositories could be gathered together to discuss and share their acquisition policies. Areas of competition and documentary gaps could be identified. Second, with a written statement of the documentary gaps, a series of meetings could be held with experts in the topics of these gaps to determine their impressions about the extent of the problem and to draw on their knowledge and experience to develop

Table 3-2: Potential Steps for Local Documentation Planning

1. Evaluate/share repository aquisition policies

2. Identify documentary gaps

3. Develop potential solutions to resolve the documentary gaps

4. Draft a working plan for documenting the locality

5. Continued evaluation and planning for local documentation

---

draft solutions. Third, armed with this more detailed information, the representatives of the institutional archives and collecting programs could draft a working plan for the more thorough documentation of the city of Pittsburgh and prepare policies for reducing or eliminating areas of competition. Such an effort, which would admittedly take at least a year and a large number of meetings and written drafts, would eventually pay off in more systematic and meaningful appraisal and documentation work.

These final examples, only briefly described here, are meant to illustrate the use, and the potential, of the documentation strategy for urban historians and researchers and archivists concerned with documenting the city. The clearest feature of the documentation strategy approach that should be noted here is that these are all *planned* efforts. Archivists and historians have long seemed to grasp onto a naturalistic view that adequate documentation of urban society (and other aspects) will result from the work of the many archival programs that have been created and have evolved through the years. But the natural results are far different. Daniel Boorstin once wrote that the "historian can rediscover the past only by the relics it has left for the present," and that the "remaining evidence of the whole human past" is "partial," "casual," and "accidental."[38] Certainly some documentation will continue to be saved in this manner, but it should be obvious that the increasing volume and complexity of information and use of computers to create and store this information requires that some better selection process than chance and accident be used. The archival documentation strategy concept is a major contribution to the development of such a process, one that guarantees a better role for the historian and other researchers as well. As one archivist recently suggested, documentation strategies

> involve a wide range of nonarchivists to provide expertise, promote and sustain a documentation project, and increase the likelihood of its success. If successful, documentation strategies establish ongoing mechanisms, not only to coordinate the collection of archival records, but to promote, support, and sustain better documentation.[39]

CASE STUDY TWO: DOCUMENTING A REGION (WESTERN NEW YORK)

TESTING THE DOCUMENTATION STRATEGY PROCESS

For some archivists the documentation strategy has just become another trendy phrase, suffering the usual mixed results by such use. In the case of documentation strategy, however, most of the reasons for its sudden emergence are good and the potential results from the strategy's use and discussion about its applications appear to be excellent. The interest in the documentation strategy seems to be directly related to archivists' general uneasiness with how effective they have been in identifying and selecting records having continuing value.

These concerns, and the efforts to resolve them, are signs of a healthy profession. For too long, archivists have been prone to define their worlds and, consequently their responsibilities, by institutional parameters. Although records are obviously created by individuals and individual institutions, these records are affected by many external influences. Archivists are now asking more and better questions that consider such influences. Instead of just asking what it is that any repository should collect, archivists are also asking questions about how they can document society, leading to cooperative efforts in analysis, planning, and action—such as those suggested by the documentation strategy.

Although the documentation strategy has been more than adequately defined,[40] several points should be kept in mind when reading the following description of its test in documenting localities. First, the documentation strategy was developed to deal with some of the serious concerns already mentioned. Second, it is not intended to replace methods of archival appraisal, but is meant to supplement these methods. Third, the documentation strategy is somewhat hypothetical at this point because it is generally untested. On the other hand, there is little substantive evaluation of the utility of generally accepted archival appraisal concepts such as evidential and informational.

THE BACKGROUND OF THE REGIONAL TEST

The Western New York documentation strategy case study described here was part of the New York Historical Records Program Development Project, funded by the National Historical Publications and Records Commission, and administered by the New York State Archives and Records Administration. The project originated with a major state-wide assessment of historical records and historical records programs in New York in 1982-83. One major conclusion of this assessment was that historical records programs lacked coordination in collecting records and that it was uncertain how well the Empire State, even with over two thousand repositories holding millions of documents, was being documented. It was acknowledged that some kind of coordinated and cooperative collecting was necessary to rectify these problems,[41] and the Western New York project was an effort to experiment with solutions to these problems.

The New York State Archives and Records Administration decided on a regional test to evaluate potential mechanisms for effectively documenting the entire state. New York was seen as too large and complex to tackle all at once. It was also assumed that documentation approaches used successfully on the regional level would probably be useful for the entire state. The state's six western counties were selected because of the presence of a variety of historical records programs, archivists and other historical records custodians and records users, a rich and diverse history, and a regional institution—the Western New York Library Resources Council, that could support such documentation analysis, planning, and implementation.[42] The Albany-based staff of the New York Historical Records Program Development Project served as the staff for the Western New York effort—that translated to be a portion of my time over a little less than two years with advice and guidance from other members of the state archives.

There were at least five questions the Western New York project was intended to answer about documentation.

- How well were regions of the state being documented through existing archival practices?
- Could the documentation strategy be used, or adapted, to help historical records programs and others evaluate and strengthen a geographical area's documentation?
- How could repositories be persuaded to revise their acquisition policies and records creators to create archival programs to ensure that the adequate documentation is created and retained?
- What kind of documentation procedures needed to be developed for documenting all of New York?
- What would the project inform the archival profession about the documentation strategy's effectiveness in documenting society?

The project provided partial conclusions to these questions; some of the lessons learned have been incorporated into the previous chapters and, especially, the final chapter on a mechanism for documenting localities.

THE STEPS IN THE TEST

The initial step in starting this project was to assemble an advisory group to analyze the quality of documentation in Western New York. The group consisted of archivists, historians and other researchers, librarians, officially appointed local historians, and the director of a regional service agency assisting local historical societies and organizations. All of these individuals were selected because of their knowledge of, and interest in, the history of Western New York. They also represented a fairly even distribution throughout the six counties, although the major metropolitan area—Buffalo—was more represented.

While this group was being assembled, a tentative framework was developed that could be used for regional documentation analysis and planning. This framework included several major parts. Fifteen topics, encompassing the entire spectrum of human activity, were identified, based on an anthropological conceptualization that had been used fairly successfully by several state archival institutions for evaluation of their acquisition programs.[43] The framework also included a simple time axis of past, present, and future that was intended to allow suitable investigation of documentation for the region's historical development *and* encouraged the working group to look to the needs of documenting the more recent past. Finally, definitions of topical significance and documentation quality were developed to assist the working group to evaluate the significance of the topics to their particular region and the quality of documentation currently held by Western New York repositories, institutional archives, and major records creators for each topic.[44]

The group met six times from Spring 1987 to Summer 1988 and discussed the nature of documentation in Western New York, the process of evaluating it, the actual nature and quality of documentation in Western New York, and the tools and products needed for guiding such geographically based documentation analysis and planning. Although the group commenced with the goal of actually producing a written plan for the improved documentation of New York's western counties and beginning an implementation of that plan, the group did not achieve either objective. In hindsight, it is fair to state that these were unrealistic objectives for a process that was new to these individuals, untested in the archival community, and that perhaps stretched the limits of the documentation strategy (especially considering that many tools as well as experience were then lacking). We discovered that a region equalled the world in its complexity. Still, some lessons were learned and major benefits gained from the work that was done.

CONCLUSIONS OF THE REGIONAL TEST

Participants in the working group concluded that the documentation process was very helpful for evaluating the collecting work of historical records repositories *and* for opening channels of communication and building bridges of cooperation between historical records repositories and users. Several members of the working group referred to the process as an excellent "consciousness raising exercise," even if it seemed overly subjective at times, that drew needed attention to the overall documentation of Western New York, a matter not being looked at carefully enough by the existing configuration of repositories and individuals. Underlying the participants' thoughts seemed to be the notion that this is a process that, although worth doing, requires significant effort and discussion to accomplish. The failure to develop a full documentation plan was counterbalanced by the recognition that a good start had been made.

The working group also recognized that they, and any other similar group, needed better procedures or guidelines for conducting geographically focused documentation analysis. This recognition shifted the group's attention to discussing what these procedures or guidelines needed to be. The New York State Archives, working with the group, developed a local documentation guide that describes the goals, benefits, and procedures of such work. This guide was produced only as a "working draft," although it has formed the foundation for Chapter 4 of this volume. The state archives intended to test the guide, to encourage others to use it and comment about its use, and eventually to issue it in a final format or abandon it in favor of some other approach to improving documentation. However, administrators at this state archives never followed up on these intentions and have remained convinced that the New York test was inconclusive (for whatever reason, broad documentation approaches have receded from the priorities of this premier state government archives).

The working group was also very helpful in suggesting ways of refining some of the original tools prepared for regional documentation analysis and planning. The group's members argued, for example, that a focus on the distant past was less helpful than one on more recent time periods. This especially caused a change in my own thinking. I assumed that individuals and institutional representatives involved in such a process would be uncomfortable in conceptualizing about documentation unless they started with older time periods and records, because this seems to be the orientation of most historical records repositories and the majority of researchers. The consensus of the Western New York working group was that there is little that can be done now to improve society's documentation prior to the twentieth century, and that attention and energy are better devoted to documenting the twentieth century, especially the post-WWII period. This attitude is partly the result of the trepidation about the massive quantities of records being produced in the late twentieth century and how these records can be properly evaluated and managed. One of the historians even expressed concern about the twentieth century becoming another "dark ages," with a paucity of surviving or understandable documentation and, therefore, a lack of understanding of our time by future generations.

The Western New York working group also struggled with the subject significance criteria proposed. The participants thought they were too imprecise. More importantly, some of the group's members felt that the criteria suggested a faulty hierarchy of historical causation. To them, the criteria suggested that one area of human activity might be more important than another; for example, that the arts were of greater value than industry or science. I must admit that I *still* struggle with this as well. The original purpose of the criteria was to identify areas of activity that were particularly important to the region's development and nature, not to suggest any general importance of one aspect of human endeavor over another. More research and experimentation need to be done. We somehow need to be able to identify areas of priority documentation action. The benefit of the criticism of the working group here, however, was to reinforce the importance of seeking a broad and even documentation of any geographical region; that is, ensuring that all major aspects of human activity are sufficiently documented (at the least, represented) by the records preserved in historical records repositories and institutional archives.

Although it was not difficult dealing with the definition of the geographical region (any definition can be accepted as long as the definition's limitations are taken in account in documentation analysis and planning), using a geographical region as the basis for documentation work caused some problems. Assembling a working group to examine all human activity in a given region eliminated the participation of records creators. The involvement of records creators is one of the major benefits of the documentation strategy approach as proposed. Applied to the geographical region, however, the approach does not really accommodate the involvement of records creators until a group turns its attention to specific topics identified as priorities for the adequate documentation of the region. How serious a problem this really is is uncertain, but it is certainly something that requires further thought and reflection. The broad documentation analysis also stretched the knowledge of the working group members. Although other experts could be consulted, or added to the group, as necessary, seeking to document a region was akin to trying to document the world. Wrestling with such problems caused several members of the working group to criticize the process as providing little more than informed intuition in making decisions about what to document and what records were needed for such documentation.

We also learned in Western New York that obtaining the resources to support broad regional documentation analysis is a difficult problem to resolve. I am still hopeful that geographical documentation work can satisfactorily be done without significant infusions of new funds; in fact, I am convinced that such work requires the support of existing historical records programs and other institutions. Given the problems of design and implementation of institutionally based acquisition policies described in Chapter 2, it is nevertheless clear that the archival profession and its constituencies must move to incorporate such documentation analysis into their standard operations. The issue remains, however, that some repository or individual must assume responsibility for coordinating such documentation analysis and planning—calling meetings, developing agendas, preparing reports, contacting needed experts, and the like. The question of resources is uncertain because the complete process was not carried through. Still to be determined is whether, in the long run, the process is cost-efficient, can generate whatever external support is needed, and the expended resources are offset by better informed selection and acquisition decisions.

ADDITIONAL QUESTIONS ABOUT THE ARCHIVAL DOCUMENTATION STRATEGY

All these problems and concerns affirm that the documentation strategy approach is a very new way for archivists, other records custodians, records users, and others to consider the selection of historical records. Concepts such as evidential and informational values and tools such as acquisition policies have had a life span of half a century or more, and they still have not been completely integrated into the archival profession and its repositories. Such documentation analysis and planning requires significant discussion and will take a long time for individuals and institutions to become accustomed to using. As such, a number of important questions remain about this approach to documenting our society.

Is the local geographical area the best way of analyzing the existing documentation and planning for the better documentation of society? Can we document society through a variety of methods—national groups focusing on specific topics, state and local groups looking at the documentation of their geographical areas, and repositories taking leadership to develop cooperative acquisition approaches with other repositories?

My response is that the locality, as discussed in this volume, is an extremely attractive focus for such documentation analysis and work for all the reasons already considered.

What is the best way of educating historical records repositories and records creators about the need for such broad-based cooperative documentation analysis and planning? Are there other approaches that might be better than the documentation strategy for working with records creators? What kinds of incentives are required?

It seems that the archival profession has failed to develop strategies for encouraging the creation of viable institutional archives, although it is absolutely clear that the prospects for successful documentation using collecting programs are nearly impossible. As to archivists, it is clear that the lack of educational opportunities for appraisal theory, methods, and practice is another reason for some of the criticism and debate about the documentation strategy.

Can such documentation analysis and planning only be undertaken if there are sources of external funds, or can such efforts be supported through the existing resources of the participants of such efforts?

As mentioned above, there is a necessity to have such approaches built into regularly supported work of institutions if there is to be successful appraisal work. This is especially important for repositories with local documentation objectives.

In any given geographical area, is there the need to include all repositories in documentation analysis and planning? Or, should it only be the major repositories involved in such efforts?

The answer to these questions probably depends on the nature of the geographical area, the array of archival and historical manuscript repositories, and the aims of the documentary work. Further work, experience, and analysis will tell the archival community what it needs to know in carrying out local documentation planning.

How do you reconcile the need to save historical records in immediate danger with the need to plan carefully for the adequate documentation of any given area?

This is a particular concern for local documentation efforts since much of what actually occurs is salvage appraisal: a company closes and its records will be destroyed; a family cleans out its garage and the family papers will be tossed if not acquired by a repository; or an organization moves from its old facility to a new structure and the older records are threatened with destruction. The problem is that such salvage appraisal has driven all or most local documentation efforts. Developing structured plans and better acquisition policies will enable repositories to make better decisions about such threats to the historical record.

Even if the documentation strategy model as now proposed is flawed, don't archivists need some kind of method that enables us to look at the broader issues of identification and selection of historical records?

Yes. Without such a method, it is difficult for archivists to see what all their efforts have added up to in regards to a comprehensive, balanced, or representative documentation of the past.

These and other questions will only be answered as archivists use the documentation strategy. For the strategy to move from a trendy phrase in the 1980s to an important process in the 1990s, the documentation strategy requires application and discussion about its use. Even if the documentation strategy is abandoned, some other process is likely to replace it since the strategy is addressing fundamental questions and problems facing the archival profession. I believe the Western New York project was only a preliminary effort at the kind of evaluation that is needed. The lessons learned from this effort, and from discussions with others in Milwaukee and other localities who have conducted such appraisal work, have been used to write the next chapter, which presents a methodology for carrying out local documentation analysis, planning, and implementation.

NOTES

1. Nancy E. Peace, "Deciding What to Save: Fifty Years of Theory and Practice," in *Archival Choices: Managing the Historical Record in an Age of Abundance,* ed. Nancy E. Peace (Lexington, MA: Lexington Books, 1984), pp. 1-18; Richard J. Cox and Helen W. Samuels, "The Archivist's First Responsibility: A Research Agenda to Improve the Identification and Retention of Records of Enduring Value," *American Archivist* 51 (Winter/Spring 1988): 28-42. See also the preceding chapter in this volume.

2. There continues to be some discussion about the decentralization of institutional and governmental archival programs, whereby the main archives stores some records but primarily provides guidance to the records creators for what records should be kept, how they should be maintained, and where and how researchers can get access to these records. This kind of operation may be necessary for some variety of electronic records, especially those that are being continually updated by their creators. Decentralization does not mean that the archivist will not conduct appraisal or perform other basic archival functions, but it simply suggests that these functions will not be carried out in a custodial environment.

3. "Society and the Formation of a Documentary Heritage: Issues in the Appraisal of Archival Sources," *Archivaria* 24 (Summer 1987): 76; this article originally appeared as "Gesellschaftsordnung und Uberlieferungsbildung: Zur Problematik archivartischer Quellenbewertung," *Archivalische Zeitschrift* 68 (1972): 3-40.

4. William L. Joyce, "The Evolution of the Concept of Special Collections in American Research Libraries," *Rare Books & Manuscripts Librarianship* 3 (Spring 1988): 19-29.

5. Tom Nesmith, "Archives From the Bottom Up: Social History and Archival Scholarship," *Archivaria* 14 (Summer 1982): 5-26; Fredric Miller, "Social History and Archival Practice," *American Archivist* 44 (Spring 1981): 113-24.

6. Warren R. Hofstra, "Community Studies: A Real World and the Academic Historian," *History News* 47 (November/December 1992): 19-23.

7. See, for example, Richard J. Cox, "A Reappraisal of Municipal Records in the United States," *Public Historian* 3 (Winter 1981): 49-63 and Peter A. Baskerville and Chad M. Gaffield, "The Crisis in Urban Documentation: 'The Shame of the Cities' Revisited," *Urban History Review* 13 (June 1984): 1-7.

8. There is no general assessment of museum archives, but a sense of what has occurred in this area can be seen in *Federal*

Funding for Museum Archives Development Programs: A Report to the Commission, Commission Reports and Papers no. 2 (Washington, DC: National Archives and Records Administration, December 1988). For an effort to portray the lack of development of public library archives, see Richard J. Cox and Anne S. K. Turkos, "Establishing Public Library Archives," *Journal of Library History* 21 (Summer 1986): 574-84.

9. Quoted in Joel Tarr, Thomas Finholt, and David Goodman, "The City and The Telegraph: Urban Telecommunications in the Pre-Telephone Era," *Journal of Urban History* 14 (November 1987): 55.

10. "Documenting Modern Cities: The Philadelphia Model," *Public Historian* 5 (Spring 1983): 78-79.

11. David Bearman, *Archival Methods, Archives and Museum Informatics Technical Report* 3 (Spring 1989), p. 9.

12. His paper was published as "The Shame of the Cities: Public Records of the Metropolis," *Midwestern Archivist* 2, no. 2 (1977): 27, 29.

13. Roy S. Dickens, Jr. and William R. Bowen, "Problems and Promises in Urban Historical Archaeology: The MARTA Project," *Historical Archaeology* 14 (1980): 51.

14. See Timothy Ericson's paper, "With a Little Imagination: Documentation Strategies in a Broader Context," unpublished paper presented to the State Historical Records Coordinators, Washington, D.C., November 2, 1989. Ericson uses the state assessment reports on the condition of historical records as a jumping off point for considering the potential of the documentation strategy concept.

15. For examples of this kind of confusion, see Connell Gallagher, "Problems of the Collection Development Archivist," *AB Bookman's Weekly* (March 19, 1990): 1225-29 and Ellen Garrison, "The Very Model of A Modern Major General: Documentation Strategy and the Center for Popular Music," *Provenance* 7 (Fall 1989): 22-32.

16. "The Archival Edge," *American Archivist* 38 (January 1975): 8.

17. "New Appraisal Techniques: The Effect of Theory on Practice," *Provenance* 7 (Fall 1989): 9.

18. See, for example, Bruce H. Bruemmer and Sheldon Hochheiser, *The High-Technology Company: A Historical Research and Archival Guide* (Minneapolis, MN: Charles Babbage Institute, Center for the History of Information Processing, University of Minnesota, 1989) and JoAnne Yates, "Internal Communication Systems in American Business: A Framework to Aid Appraisal," *American Archivist* 48 (Spring 1985): 141-51.

19. Advisory Committee for the Co-ordination of Information Systems, *Management of Electronic Records: Issues and Guidelines* (New York: United Nations, 1990).

20. "Society of American Archivists Guidelines for Graduate Archival Education Programs," *American Archivist* 51 (Summer 1988): 380-89.

21. Hedstrom, "New Appraisal Techniques," 3-7;

22. *Reading the Popular* (Boston: Unwin Hyman, 1989), pp. 1-2, 6.

23. *Time Passages: Collective Memory and American Popular Culture* (Minneapolis: University of Minnesota Press, 1990), p. 36.

24. William Sharpe and Leonard Wallock, "From 'Great Town' to 'Nonplace Urban Realm': Reading the Modern City," in *Visions of the Modern City: Essays in History, Art, and Literature*, eds. Sharpe and Wallock (New York: Proceedings of the Hyman Center for the Humanities, Columbia University, [1983]), p. 8.

25. "The Philadelphia Social History Project: A Methodological History," Stanford University, 1973 Ph.D. dissertation, p. 365.

26. See, for example, Samuel Hays, ed., *City at the Point: Essays on the Social History of Pittsburgh* (Pittsburgh, PA: University of Pittsburgh Press, 1989).

27. Michael H. Ebner, "The Comparative Tradition in American Urban History," *Journal of Interdisciplinary History* 17 (Winter 1987), 639-43. For the sociological perspective on comparison, see S.N. Eisenstadt and A. Shachar, *Society, Culture, and Urbanization* (Newbury Park, CA: Sage Publications, 1987).

28. Kathleen Neils Conzen, "Quantification and the New Urban History," *Journal of Interdisciplinary History* 13 (Spring 1983), 661.

29. W. Parker Frisbie, "Urban Sociology in the United States: The Past 20 Years," *American Behavioral Scientist* 24 (November/December 1980): 177-214.

30. See Leith Mullings, ed., *Cities of the United States: Studies in Urban Anthropology* (New York: Columbia University Press, 1987), especially Mullings introductory chapter.

31. "Urban Folklore: A Behavioral Approach," *Western Folklore* 38, no. 3 (1979), 158-59.

32. Janet Langlois and Philip LaRonge, "Using a Folklore Archive," in *Handbook of American Folklore*, ed. Richard M. Dorson (Bloomington: Indiana University Press, 1983), p. 392.

33. Barbara Clark Smith, "The Authority of History: The Changing Public Face of the Historical Society of Pennsylvania," *Pennsylvania Magazine of History and Biography* 114 (January 1990): 64. Other essays in this volume about the exhibition are by Gary B. Nash, Emma J. Lapsansky, and Cynthia Jeffress Little and provide,

as a group, an illuminating exploration of the use of material culture and other historical records in public exhibitions.

34. "The Roots of 128: A Hypothetical Documentation Strategy," *American Archivist* 50 (Fall 1987): 526.

35. The ad hoc approach can be seen in John A. Fleckner and Stanley Mallach, eds., *Guide to Historical Resources in Milwaukee Area Archives* (Milwaukee: Milwaukee Area Archives Group, 1976).

36. The institutional collection analysis approach is described in Judith E. Endelman, "Looking Backward to Plan for the Future: Collection Analysis for Manuscript Repositories," *American Archivist* 50 (Summer 1987): 340-55.

37. Timothy A. Slavin, "A Documentation Strategy for a Catholic Diocese: Testing the Documentation Strategy," paper presented at the 1989 Society of American Archivists meeting, St. Louis, Missouri.

38. *Hidden History* (New York: Harper and Row, 1987), pp. 3-4.

39. Hedstrom, "New Appraisal Techniques," 11.

40. Helen W. Samuels, "Who Controls the Past," *American Archivist* 49 (Spring 1986): 109-24; Larry J. Hackman and Joan Warnow-Blewett, "The Documentation Strategy Process: A Model and A Case Study," *American Archivist* 50 (Winter 1987): 12-47; and Philip N. Alexander and Helen W. Samuels, "The Roots of 128: A Hypothetical Documentation Strategy," *American Archivist* 50 (Fall 1987): 518-31.

41. *Toward A Usable Past: Historical Records in the Empire State* (Albany: New York Historical Records Advisory Board, 1984).

42. The actual configuration of counties was determined by the system of nine regional library research and resource councils. These councils, with two decades of service to libraries, were likely choices for sponsoring such documentation work because of their experience with regions, existing mechanisms to coordinate cooperative efforts, and, in the case of a number of regions, their interest in archives and historical records.

43. For a description of such efforts, refer to Judith E. Endelman, "Looking Backward to Plan for the Future: Collection Analysis for Manuscript Repositories," *American Archivist* 50 (Summer 1987): 340-55. The topics included agriculture; arts and architecture; business, industry, and manufacturing; education; environmental affairs and natural resources; labor; medicine and health care; military; politics, government, and law; populations; recreation and leisure; religion; science and technology; social organization and activity; and transportation and communication.

44. These scales were modelled after those developed in the RLG Conspectus project. Copies of the scales can be acquired from the New York State Archives and Records Administration or viewed in

the collection of readings assembled for use in the documentation strategy seminars sponsored by the Society of American Archivists in 1987 to 1991.

4

DOCUMENTING LOCALITIES:
A PRACTICAL APPROACH

This chapter provides a practical description of a mechanism that could be used to assist archival institutions and other organizations and groups to plan and implement local documentation activities. A concise series of actions is described that can assist in the determination of what is needed to be known about localities and what kinds of records are essential to their effective documentation. While not meant to be a prescriptive solution, it is proposed as an alternative approach to documenting localities. The documentation process described here emphasizes multi-institutional cooperating rather than relying upon individual archival programs, the establishing of institutional archival programs rather than solely depending upon collecting by historical manuscripts programs, and setting specific objectives for acquiring documentation rather than merely trusting achieving an adequate documentation by analyzing existing records, often fragmentary in nature. The resources, time, and energy required for implementing these recommendations depend on the complexity and nature of the geographic area being documented, as well as the documentary goals.

The original concepts described here evolved from a Western New York test of the documentation strategy undertaken as part of a special project of the New York State Archives and Records Administration, in coordination with the Western New York Library Resources Council and the New York State Historical Records Advisory Board. Most of what appears here is the result of considerable modification which emanated from the author's participation in a series of workshops from 1987 through 1991 on archival documentation strategies, co-taught with Timothy Ericson and Helen Samuels.

WHAT IS A DOCUMENTED LOCALITY?

For the purposes of this chapter, documenting a locality means ensuring that the essential aspects of a community's past and present—such as significant topics, events, and trends and movements—are adequately represented by records selected for preservation and that these records are accessible to researchers. The concept of "adequacy of documentation" has been used by the National Archives, although briefly and not very convincingly, in its efforts to reconceptualize its mission in light of the vastly transforming information environment that characterizes the federal government. The National Archives' use of this concept seems to have been as a synonym for "accountability." As the single published article on adequacy of documentation stated it,

> Although much has been written on the need to efficiently manage and distribute information collected by the government, information managers have not focused much effort on the need to create adequate information, or more properly records, to make accountability possible. Stated differently, information managers have been more concerned with gathering, processing, and disseminating information without examining the purposes served by creating the record in the first place.[1]

Adequacy of local documentation is intended to mean more than accountability, as I have suggested. Significance and representativeness are more crucial to this notion.

There are other important elements as well. The prospects of achieving an adequately documented locality are dependent on the cooperation of a variety of institutions and individuals, as will be described in the following paragraphs. Institutional archives must be encouraged as a normative process. Collecting programs must reformulate their acquisition policies to take into account the larger objective of documenting the locality. Moreover, in many cases, these collecting programs must consider their priority to be that of serving as a repository of last resort; that is, they accept historical manuscripts or archival records only when there is no prospects for the preservation of these materials through the creation of an institutional program or acceptance by another appropriate repository, *and* the records have been determined to be crucial to the locality's documentation. Furthermore, the adequate documentation of a locality may also require cooperation with other agencies, such as museums and historic sites, because the preservation of artifacts and other material remains of the locality, along with oral history and folklore sources, may be necessary for achieving desired ends.

In conducting local documentation work, it is always essential for the leaders and architects of such plans to remember that they are imposing order on, for want of a better term, chaos, or what appears to be chaotic. James Beniger provides the relevant point in his *Control Revolution* when he compares organization and order. For the comparison he moves from crystals, with their "regularity and repetition" (order) to the amoeba, lacking order, "a formless bag full of sticky fluid in which irregularly shaped molecules float haphazardly." The locality must seem like the amoeba, but, Beniger reminds us, the "amoeba is highly organized."[2] Hence, archivists and their allies should not refrain from trying to impose order; it is there in the structure of society on the local level, waiting to be discovered.

GETTING A LOCAL DOCUMENTATION PROJECT STARTED

Starting such a project requires either an institution or an individual taking the initiative to bring together other institutions and individuals interested in the documentation work. Given the efforts of most locally oriented historical manuscripts, archives, history, and library programs, such initiatives should almost occur naturally, although they obviously have not normally occurred in this manner. But it is important to realize that local documentation projects can be commenced by any number of groups or individuals, including the following.

- Staff of a historical records repository, such as a historical society, public library, museum, or local government archives.
- Local historians.
- Other users of local historical and archival records, such as academically based historians, social scientists, political scientists, and so forth.
- Representatives of regional studies centers located at universities and colleges.
- Representatives of groups concerned about the collection, preservation, and use of historical records, such as historic preservation groups and educational institutions.
- Creators of important records, such as business and corporate figures.

Conducting local documentation work should not require significant financial resources. It does require individuals and their institutions to commit *time* to meetings and to the ongoing refinement and implementation of a plan for adequately documenting the locality. Local community funding sources—such as foundations, corporate givers, and individual benefactors—might provide additional financial support because of the importance of the work, the public interest that can be generated by these efforts, and the likely participation of many records creators, custodians, and users. The lack of financial prospects should not deter such documentation analysis, planning, and actions from taking place, and this work should be built into the normal ongoing operations of most archival and historical records programs. In fact, excellent work can be accomplished through the pooling of resources, primarily time and expertise, from participants in such efforts.

Although the various steps described here are provided to guide institutions and individuals in the documentation of localities, variations may be required due to differing characteristics of geographic areas, historical records and archival repositories, records creators, and potential actors in the documentation process. However the steps are used, the effectiveness of the local documentation effort is dependent on an ongoing commitment to implement and continually refine the documentation plan. Just as a locality is in a state of continuous change, however imperceptible at any given moment, the effort to document the locality must consider this change and be refined accordingly. Successes in identifying and preserving important archival records and historical manuscripts will also require periodic changes in the documentation plan.

There are a number of potential benefits to be obtained by following the advice in this chapter. Obviously, its use should strengthen the work of all archival and historical manuscript repositories with some interest or stake in documenting a particular locality. Following these steps can help raise the consciousness of repository staffs and governing boards and others to the needs of documenting society and the reasons for acquiring and preserving historical records. At a minimum, the use of this chapter should assist in the identification of underdocumented or neglected areas of human activity and lead to actions to correct these problems. Such analysis and cooperative work will help inform records custodians and users that the existing sets of repositories normally making up the local archival community cannot effectively acquire all the records necessary for documenting a particular locality, due to large quantity of records, space needs, maintenance costs, issues of access, and so forth.

The steps described here should assist in the complicated process of persuading records creators to establish institutional archives or to adopt other means for managing their important records. The experience of conducting such work can also lead to cooperation in other important areas, such as the joint publication of archival and historical records guides, improved storage for such records, the preparation of disaster-preparedness plans, and informing the local public about the value of the archival and historical records in their vicinity. In other words, cooperation in one area, such as documentation work, should lead to cooperation in other basic archival functions, all of which will support the aims of better documented localities.[3]

THE ESSENTIAL PRODUCTS OF LOCAL DOCUMENTATION ANALYSIS

Every local documentation project should lead to the creation of at least two products: a *written plan* to guide continuing work for the locality's documentation and a *continuing advisory group* that carries out the plan, monitors progress on it, and revises the plan to reflect the changing nature of the locality and the successes and failures in the use of the plan. Both the written plan and advisory group are essential for achieving an effective or adequate documentation of any locality.

The length and detail of a local documentation plan may vary according to the interest, energy, resources, and objectives of a documentation advisory group, but every plan should include at least five basic factors. (See Figure 4-1 for a sample format for such a plan.) These five factors support the plan's major purpose: to stimulate actions for achieving an effective documentation of the locality.

There should be a brief history of the geographic area, using the broad topics of human activity described later in this chapter, or some appropriate variation of the topical scheme to meet the locality's needs. Each topical category's features and activities should be summarized as they relate to the geographical area's development and present nature. Significant trends, events, and other characteristics can be briefly noted in the historical description, providing a means for evaluating present holdings and acquisition practices of existing historical records programs and institutional archives.

A written documentation plan should also include an evaluation of the existing documentation quality for each major topic, again later described in this chapter. Issues about information gaps in the locality's documentation

<u>Elements of Plan</u>

1.   Geographical scope/definition

2.   Documentation Advisory group (key organizations and individuals
     participating in analysis and drafting)

3.   Information and opinions desired but unavailable
     a.   data bases
     b.   written surveys and studies
     c.   on-site surveys and studies
     d.   meetings and discussions
     e.   special analyses
     f.   other sources

4.   Information and opinions desired but unavailable

5.   Summary of major findings
     a.   characteristics of historical development of the locality
     b.   evaluation and comparison of existing documentation quality and
          significance of each major topic
     c.   general recommendations of topics for priority documentation
          efforts
     d.   statement of desired documentation of the locality

6.   Recommended actions/practices for priority documentation topics:

<u>Topic</u>	<u>Suggested Actors and Actors</u>	<u>Role of documenta-tion work-ing group</u>
1.		
2.		
3.		
etc.		

7.   Date this report issued:

8.   Target date for next revision:

Figure 4-1. Plan for Documenting a Geographical Area: Sample Format

should also be discussed in the report since they may represent problems in the selection of topical areas for further documentation analysis and may need to be resolved in the future.

A documentation plan should highlight topical areas that are considered to be under-documented and extremely significant to the geographical area's development and present nature or that require more careful investigation. The plan should describe what such efforts will require in terms of additional advisory groups, repositories and actors, and resources.

The plan should also include a brief discussion of what the locality's documentation should look like in the future. This segment should describe the type and variety of historical records repositories, institutional and government archives, documentation advisory groups, research use, and the importance of various information sources for documenting the locality.

The report's most important part is the set of recommendations for actions in priority topical areas.[4] The advisory group, after having analyzed the general nature of the locality's development and its current documentation, should be able to select the topics that are priorities for documentation action, using at least the following criteria:

- Importance of the topic to the locality (in regard to its development and its documentation).
- Current state of and needs for the topic's documentation.
- Whether there is the proper mix of historical records repositories and institutional archives required to support the topic's documentation.
- Whether there is sufficient interest by historical records repository and institutional archives staffs, records creators, and others in documenting the topic.

The first two items represent the most important criteria. Items three and four should be a natural outcome of evaluating the condition of the locality's documentation.

AN ONGOING DOCUMENTATION ADVISORY GROUP

The main purpose of the written documentation plan is to ensure the locality's documentation; the best plan is useless if its recommendations are not acted upon. Such actions should be monitored by an *ongoing* advisory group. The specific responsibilities of such an advisory group, after the preparation of the documentation plan, include at least the following.

- Convincing records creators to originate, retain, and appropriately administer historical and archival records, by developing their own archival programs or entering into depository agreements with collecting programs.
- Encouraging collecting repositories and existing institutional archives to modify their acquisition policies and practices and to cooperate with other programs to ensure the locality's effective documentation.
- Asking records creators and repositories to report to the interested public appropriate documentation policies, practices, decisions, uses, benefits, and needs so that documentation efforts may be improved overall.
- Informing interested parties and the public of documentation conditions and needs so that they are aware of and may support the recommendations from the locality's documentation plan.
- Seeking resources needed to sustain and improve the locality's documentation.

The main objective of the advisory group is to assist the historical records repositories, records creators, and other important parties to assimilate the broader mission of documenting the locality into their own specific missions and activities. Steps to guide the initial work of the advisory group are described in the next section.

SUGGESTED BASIC STEPS FOR DOCUMENTATION ANALYSIS AND PLANNING

There are five basic steps for evaluating a locality's documentation and developing a documentation plan. (See Figure 4-2.) These steps should be considered in light of the specific needs and characteristics of the localities. Throughout the description (which has been kept in a concise form to encourage easy use) of this process, there are references to certain forms and other tools discussed elsewhere in this book.

STEP ONE: ASSEMBLE ADVISORY GROUP AND CONDUCT PRELIMINARY REVIEW OF THE LOCALITY'S DEVELOPMENT AND DOCUMENTATION

1. Assemble representatives[5] of the major historical records repositories, local government and corporate records officers, other archivists and librarians familiar with the locality's historical records and their use, and local historians and others knowledgeable about the area's history and present nature.

2. Review the purposes and goals of the local documentation effort. Use this chapter and the references cited in its bibliography as a starting point for discussion. The preparation of a brief list of documentation objectives, tailored to the locality's peculiar needs and characteristics, is useful for stimulating interest and guiding early discussion.[6]

3. Consider the primary characteristics of the locality's past development and present nature, identifying essential aspects that require documentation. Use the topical framework in this chapter and the questions in Figure 4-3 for review and discussion. If resources or volunteer services are available, prepare a brief background paper on the development and nature of the locality that can facilitate discussion by the advisory group.

4. Discuss current general perceptions of the quality of documentation, considering the present collections and acquisition policies of historical records repositories and the sufficiency of institutional and government archives in the locality. Use the questions in Figure 4-3 to guide analysis of

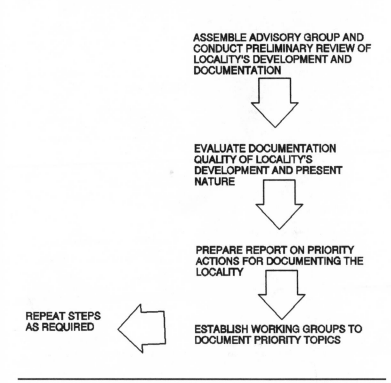

Figure 4-2. Documenting a Geographical Area: Five Basic Steps

the existing documentation's quality. Gather written acquisition policies and descriptions of the locality's historical
records holdings. If resources or the services of a volunteer
are obtainable, prepare a brief paper that generally describes
the present collections and acquisition policies of historical
records repositories and the sufficiency (in terms of coverage)
of institutional and government archives in the locality. To
facilitate discussion have members of the advisory group fill
out the documentation worksheets after the first meeting
and tabulate and disseminate the results prior to the second
meeting.[7]

Development

1. What are the reasons for the locality's historical development and when did that development begin?

2. What are the major periods of the locality's historical development?

3. What are the most important features (topics) of the locality's historical development and present nature?

4. What are the varying characteristics and nature of each of the major topics of human activity in the locality?

5. How has the locality's historical development related to and been affected by the development of other localities, regions, states, and the nation?

6. Has there been sufficient study and dissemination of the results of such study on the historical development and present nature of the locality? Does the locality have a sufficient number of regional experts and organizations to assist in its thorough documentation?

Documentation

1. Is there sufficient documentation of the locality's origins in repositories? Is there documentation known about that is not being adequately preserved int eh historical records repositories?

2. Is there sufficient documentation for each of these periods in historical records repositories? What periods are most under-represented in the repositories or by institutional archives and can these weaknesses be corrected?

3. Are there major topics adequately documented by current holdings of historical records programs and institutional archives? What are the features best and least documented and what accounts for these differences? Is there a sufficient variety of historical records programs (college and university archives, institutional archives such as businesses and civic organizations, historical societies, local public libraries, museums, and government archives) to ensure the adequate documentation of the locality?

4. Is there adequate documentation for capturing the broad range of activities that characterize the locality? Is the locality being adequately documented in a general sense?

5. Is there documentation related to the historical development of the locality in other localities, regions, and states?

6. Has that study been affected by the holdings and present acquisition policies of the locality's repositories and the quality of experts available in the locality? What are the main obstacles and problems to correcting or improving this situation?

Figure 4-3. Basic Questions for Preliminary Review of Locality's Development and Documentation

5. Reconsider and agree on the purposes and goals of the documentation evaluation and alter the advisory group as necessary to continue its work. Develop a supplemental list of experts who could be called upon for additional advice when needed. Put these purposes and goals in writing and, if possible, issue a general publicity release to build community interest and support.

STEP TWO: EVALUATE THE DOCUMENTATION QUALITY OF THE MAJOR ASPECTS OF THE LOCALITY'S HISTORICAL DEVELOPMENT AND PRESENT NATURE

1. Evaluate each topical category in the locality's historical development and present nature. This effort should assist the identification of the locality's key features requiring special attention to ensure its adequate documentation.* Draw upon the subject knowledge of the advisory group members, other experts as necessary, and existing studies on the locality's history, recent development, and present nature.[8]

2. Evaluate the nature and preservation of the locality's historical records already held by repositories for each major topic. Also consider the nature of the existence of institutional archives. Use available repository finding aids. Consider repositories outside of the locality that might hold important historical records related to it; use the Research Library Information Network (RLIN), other finding aids, and the knowledge of the advisory group to determine the nature of such historical records holdings.

3. Compare the significance of each topic to the locality's historical development with the topics' existing documentation. Discuss general impressions and investigate where necessary to identify gaps in the locality's documentation. Use the completed worksheets and the advisory group's expertise. Seek additional expert opinion for unanswered questions or unresolved problems. Compare documentation

---

* A sample worksheet has been included as Appendix A. It is intended to serve as a model for adaptation for use by individuals and institutions engaged in local documentation analysis.

gaps to the current acquisition policies of the locality's historical records repositories and institutional archives.

STEP THREE: PREPARE REPORT ON PRIORITY ACTIONS FOR DOCUMENTING THE LOCALITY

1. Prepare a brief report on the strengths and weaknesses of the locality's documentation, identifying priority actions, actors and mechanisms needed for meeting these priorities. Use information gathered during step two.

2. Disseminate the report to all historical records repositories, local historians, subject experts, historical records users, appropriate records creators, and other interested parties in the locality. Seek wide discussion of the report to stimulate interest in it and to strengthen its conclusions and recommendations. Such review can be conducted through a one-day conference, sessions at appropriate meetings of local historical, archival, and library professional associations, discussions with individuals, and a mailing with a request for comment. For a sample list of questions to use in this review, see Table 4-1.

3. Prepare and disseminate the final report and revise, if necessary, the composition of the advisory group for ongoing monitoring, evaluating, and improving the locality's documentation. The advisory group should use the final report as a basis for their continuing work and periodically issue progress reports and major revisions of the plan.[9] Issue a general publicity release to build support in the locality for documentation work.

STEP FOUR: ESTABLISH WORKING GROUPS TO ANALYZE AND PLAN FOR DOCUMENTING PRIORITY TOPICAL AREAS

1. Select one (or more) of the priority areas identified in the final documentation plan for additional analysis, planning, and implementation.[10]

2. Establish a working group similar to that described in phase one, *except* include experts, experienced records users, and records creators crucial to the topic's adequate documentation.

Table 4-1: Sample Questions for Review of Locality's Documentation Plan

1. Do you believe that this locality is being adequately documented? Do you agree with the characterization of need as presented in the draft documentation plan? Is the description of current acquisition policies and practices by historical records programs in the locality an accurate one? What records are being regularly destroyed, and what problems do such destruction present for the documentation of the locality?

2. Are there topical areas concerning this locality's history and present nature that have been significantly underdocumented? Are there topical areas that have been well-documented? Do you agree with the assessment of the draft documentation plan?

3. Does this locality have a sufficient variety of historical records and institutional archives programs to ensure its adequate documentation? Are there historical records programs successfully acquiring the records essential for documenting the locality? Do you agree with the assessment of the draft documentation plan in this area?

4. Do you agree with the priorities for further documentation analysis and planning identified in the draft documentation plan? If not, what topical areas for priority action would you recommend and why?

5. Do you have suggestions for participants in the documentation working groups being formed to carry out priority actions? Are you interested in serving on one of these groups?

6. What groups or individuals do you suggest for receiving copies of this documentation plan? What recommendations can you make for further disseminating and publicizing the plan?

3. Draft a preliminary topical documentation strategy statement and disseminate it throughout the locality to generate interest and support for the effort. This statement should clarify the scope and boundaries of the topic to be documented, and how this effort fits into the overall documentation of the locality. Use the locality's documentation

Table 4-2: Topical Documentation Strategy Statement: Sample Format

Elements of Statement

1. Topical area.
2. Geographical scope/definition.
3. Documentation working group (key organizations and individuals participating in analysis and drafting).
4. Information and opinions drawn on (describe each).
   a. data bases.
   b. written surveys and guides.
   c. meetings and discussions.
   d. Special analyses.
   e. other sources.
5. Information and opinions desired but unavailable.
6. Summary of major findings (Follow list of considerations agreed upon by documentation working group).
7. Recommended actions/practices.
8. Date this statement issued.
9. Target date for next revision.

plan completed in step three as a reference point. Use Table 4-2 as a model for developing the statement.

4. Conduct in-depth study of the topical area under consideration. Consider the following issues: the types of documentation being created; the essential information that needs to be preserved to document effectively the topical area; what historical and archival records are currently being preserved in historical records repositories and institutional archives; and what actions need to be taken to close the gap between the documentation requirements and present conditions. Use questions listed in Table 4-3.

5. Prepare written documentation statement for the topical area and begin its implementation. Follow up the preparation of the topical documentation plan with necessary actions such as encouraging repositories to change their present acquisition practices, persuading important records creators to establish archival programs, acquiring financial resources to microfilm endangered historical records crucial

Table 4-3: Questions for Developing Topical Documentation Strategies

1. What are present records practices for this topic?
    a. What records are already available in repositories?
    b. What records are being regularly accessioned by repositories on a systematic basis?
    c. What records are being sought by historical records programs but are not being accessioned regularly? Why are they being sought? Why aren't they being accessioned?
    d. What records are being retained by their creators but not sought by historical records programs? Why?
    e. What records are being regularly destroyed? Why?
2. What are past, present, and projected uses, and benefits from these uses, of records in this topic?
3. For this topic:
    a. What categories of records are worth preserving from the perspective of typical records creators?
    b. What categories of records are worth preserving from the perspective or interests of others?
    c. What records may be of interest from the perspective of the public welfare of future generations?
4. What historical records most readily lend themselves to retention through a coordinated selection from among the records of their creators?
5. What records cannot yet be evaluated for potential selection and preservation:
    a. Without knowing more about the status or records creation, administration, retention, accessioning, or use?
    b. Without knowing more about these factors beyond the locality?
    c. Without knowing more about the relationship of such records to other forms of related information?
6. Who are the major established and potential parties interested in documentation of this topic? What are their views on the current condition of documentation in this area?
7. What present policies and practices seem most detrimental to better creation, identification, retention, and treatment of historical records in the documentation area?
    a. By records creators?
    b. By historical records programs?
    c. By other parties?
8. What new policies and practices would be the most likely to improve the future condition of documentation?
9. How can records creators, existing historical records repositories, and others be influenced to act individually and collectively to refine present acquisition policies and practices in appropriate ways?
10. Which of these factors can be most effectively fostered during the next several years, and which must await attention at a later time?

to the topic, and the like. Use the sample documentation strategy format included in Table 4-2.

6. Submit the topical documentation statement to the ongoing advisory group overseeing the locality's documentation and revise the locality's general documentation plan accordingly.

7. Continue regular meetings (at least once a year) of the topical documentation working group to monitor changes and to continue work on adequate documentation of the topic.

8. Report regularly to the ongoing advisory group responsible for the locality's documentation and revise the general plan and actions necessary for documenting the locality.

STEP FIVE: CONTINUE IMPROVING LOCALITY'S DOCUMENTATION

1. Continue regular (at least twice a year) meetings of the advisory group.

2. Consider changes to the locality's documentation plan and revise the plan as necessary. Continue to promote actions needed for ensuring locality's documentation.[11]

3. Establish working groups in newly identified topical priority areas and monitor their efforts. Use this chapter and completed work as examples.

4. Issue publicity about progress in the locality's documentation through press releases, meetings of professional associations and other groups, and special conferences as appropriate.

A FRAMEWORK FOR DOCUMENTATION ANALYSIS

This section provides guidance for assessing a locality's documentation to assist historical records programs, subject experts, and others. The framework consists of criteria for determining documentation quality, both retrospectively and for current society. Using the criteria will help the preparation of the locality's documentation plan and identification of topical priorities for additional documentation analysis and implementation.

It is important to realize before using it, that the documentation framework described here is a subjective tool. Assembling an informed, active documentation advisory group is the *best* means of ensuring the locality's documentation. The locality's documentation will improve through the evaluation process, not the plan itself; the plan, being only a means to an end, does not need to be perfect.

The framework (see Table 4-4) discussed in this section has three purposes:

- It organizes human activity into manageable topics and time periods.
- It enables the assessment of the locality's documentation.
- It supports the process, described in Section Three of this guide, for evaluating and improving a locality's documentation.

The framework's most important aspect is the topical categories (defined later in this chapter). The purpose of these topics is to represent the broadest possible range of human activity that can be used for assessing and strengthening the locality's documentation.

The framework also has a time axis. Time—especially as reflected in the origins and development of institutions, events, societal groups, and so forth—is also an important consideration. To document accurately and fully any topic in a locality, it is helpful to consider the topic's beginning and development. The "past" can be generally defined as the beginning of activity in any of the topical categories, whether it occurs in the eighteenth century or the 1970s, and time's division into three phases is only for the convenience of documentation analysis. Since most early historical records have either already been collected or destroyed (and since what will turn up is likely to be saved) and since the more recent twentieth century is the most difficult time to document, the main emphasis of the process described in this chapter is on the modern period. Documentation working groups might wish, however, to revise these time periods to fit their own locality's historical development.

Table 4-4: Framework for Documenting Localities

Time Periods	Topics

(Pre-1900)
 	
20th Century
 	
Present
	Agriculture
	Arts and Architecture
	Business, Industry, Manufacturing
	Education
	Environmental Affairs and Natural
	   Resources
	Labor
	Medicine and Health Care
	Military
	Politics, Government, Law
	Populations
	Recreation and Leisure
	Religion
	Science and Technology
	Social Organization and
	   Communication

To use effectively this framework, a gauge is needed for determining documentation quality for each topic (see Table 4-5). Four levels—insignificant, minimal, moderate, and significant—are included to assess a topic's documentation quality. Although a particular topic's importance to the locality can also vary, a major aim of documenting the locality is to ensure some archival coverage of the full range of human activity within a geographic area. The emphasis should be, therefore, on the documentation quality of each topic. The four levels for documentation quality weight the collecting habits or intentions of the locality's historical records programs, suggest the potential need for institutional, corporate, and public archives, and evaluate the actual holdings of historical records repositories and archival institutions against the locality's nature.

The documentation quality scale should be used to guide the writing of brief narrative accounts on a topic's quality of documentation; the advisory group's subject experts might wish to add some comments on the importance of the topic

Table 4-5: Criteria for Topical Documentation Quality

0. Insignificant Level	No or few historical records repositories with existing collections or with policies that promote collection in this topic; no organizational, institutional, or corporate archives related to this topic.
1. Minimal Level	Repositories have some collections related to the topic, but with major gaps in the topic's documentation; repository acquisition policies do not emphasize the collection of records related to the topic; few organizational, institutional, or corporate archives pertaining to the topic.
2. Moderate Level	Significant repository holdings (in quantity and quality), but still uneven in topic's coverage; repository acquisition policies cover the collection of records related to major, but not all, aspects of the topics; some organizational, institutional, and corporate archives complement other collecting repositories, such as historical societies and libraries.
3. Significant Level	Important repository collections (in quantity and quality) covering all elements of the topic; repository acquisitions emphasize all crucial aspects of the topic; adequate organizational, institutional, and corporate archives that complement other collecting repositories.

to the locality that can assist in the determination of priorities for action. The narrative reports should primarily be descriptions of the nature of a specific subject in that locality with its assigned rate of documentation quality. This type of exercise will help to determine *general* needs for action, primarily through the advisory body's discussion and preliminary evaluation. This analysis can help guide decision making about when and where to invest additional resources to document the locality.

DEFINITIONS OF TOPICS OF HUMAN ACTIVITY FOR DOCUMENTATION

This section provides additional information on fifteen major topics, covering the broad spectrum of human activity. These topics are designed to assist archivists, librarians, local historians, and other interested parties in documenting a locality and have been derived from other macroappraisal efforts carried out by archival programs since the mid-1980s.[12] For this reason, the definitions of these topics are reflected on the worksheets. More precise descriptions of a topic in a particular locality will eventually be necessary, and at that point, topical and geographical experts should be sought for additional advice. More precise definitions should come from the documentation process underway in the locality, reflecting the needs for documenting the locality rather than from some rigid external sources such as library subject classifications.

There are obvious overlaps between the topics. "Labor" is crucial to "Business, Industry and Manufacturing" and vice versa. Local working groups must determine their documentation needs and effectively cross-reference their findings between the major topics. These topics are only meant to *guide* local documentation analysis and action, not to determine rigidly every detail of such work. Users of this guide should not be bound to the specifics of these topical definitions, but should work on those aspects most important to the adequate documentation of their locality.

Each topic includes a brief, general definition with some description of the varieties of records crucial for its documentation. There are also citations to articles and books, if any, that describe the use of various types of records; this literature might be useful to the advisory group seeking to document a topic.

The information below does not include detailed descriptions of the nature of records needing preservation in order to document adequately each subject. The chapter's brevity makes this impossible, although citations to publications providing additional information have been included. In general, business records, institutional and organizational archives, personal and family papers, oral interviews, and local, state, and federal government records will be essential to documenting every topic. Users of this chapter should review the general bibliography on historical records appraisal and documentation included in chapter five for additional guidance.

Individuals seeking to document their locality should also be aware that records important for this purpose may reside in repositories in other locations. There are historical records programs, for example, that collect on a statewide basis or that have records of statewide significance. Some national repositories, like the National Archives and Records Administration and the Library of Congress, also may hold historical records with information vital for documenting a specific locality. Although local documentation working groups should not over stress the importance of such records when they labor to document their areas, these groups should be at least aware of these information sources.

THE TOPICS

AGRICULTURE

Agriculture is the production, processing, and promotion of agricultural commodities, ranging from small-scale family farms to large-scale commercial operations. Important archives and manuscripts include those documenting research in horticulture, animal husbandry, and other agricultural sciences; family and corporate farming; commercial establishments and cooperatives; transportation and marketing corporations; agricultural economics; groups formed to lobby, educate, or promote about or for agricultural issues and concerns, such as agricultural societies, agricultural fairs, and professional agricultural organizations; and individuals prominent in agricultural affairs.

There are few useful descriptions of the nature of agricultural records. A good starting point is Gould P. Colman, "Documenting Agriculture and Rural Life," *Midwestern Archivist* 12, no. 1 (1987): 21-27, an article which describes the work of Cornell University. Another useful essay is Samuel A. McReynolds, "Rural Life in New England," *American Archivist* 50 (Fall 1987): 532-48.

ARTS AND ARCHITECTURE

Arts and architecture encompasses the production, promotion, and sponsorship of visual and graphic arts, performing arts, folk arts, literature, music, architecture, and any other activities ranging from fine arts to entertainment. Important archives and manuscripts include those of individual artists, architects, and writers; institutions and organizations supporting or promoting such activities, including foundations and museums; entertainment companies; and architectural firms.

Few analyses about the documentation of the arts and architecture have appeared. Nancy Carlson Shrock, "Images of New England: Documenting the Built Environment," *American Archivist* 50 (Fall 1987): 474-98 is a superb introduction to documenting architecture in a geographic area, although there little evidence that her approach has been followed. Individuals interested in this topic might also look at William Deiss, *Museum Archives: An Introduction* (Chicago: Society of American Archivists, 1984); this manual provides a useful description of the kinds of records that museums should maintain to document their own activities. Other useful references on architectural records include Alan K. Lathrop's writings, "The Provenance and Preservation of Architectural Records," *American Archivist* 43 (Summer 1980): 325-38; "Appraisal and Accessioning of Architectural

Records," *Proceedings of the Conference Toward Standards for Architectural Archives* (Washington, DC: American Institute of Architects Foundation, 1984), pp. 33-40; "The Archivist and Architectural Records," *Georgia Archive* 5 (Summer 1977): 25-33; and "Copyright of Architectural Records: A Legal Perspective," *American Archivist* 49 (Fall 1986): 409-23. Lathrop, in his writings, has urged an appraisal focus on "major stylistic schools of architecture" and firms with long existences, recipients of design honors, and those businesses possessing a considerable quantity of their firms' records. Another standard reference source is Ralph E. Ehrenberg, *Archives & Manuscripts: Maps and Architectural Drawings* (Chicago: Society of American Archivists, 1982). A rare, focused case study in the appraisal of architectural records is Kathleen Mallon, "The Chicago Historical Society and the Records of Henry Weese and Associates: Appraisal of Current Architectural Records," *Proceedings of the Conference Toward Standards for Architectural Archives* (Washington, DC: American Institute of Architects Foundation, 1984), pp. 41-51; Mallon's essay, while not focused on broader documentary values, is a solid introduction to the process of evaluation for specific types of architectural records. Philip N. Cronenwett, "Appraisal of Literary Manuscripts," in *Archival Choices: Managing the Historical Record in an Age of Abundance,* ed. Nancy E. Peace (Lexington, MA: D. C. Heath, 1984), pp. 105-16 is a reasonable introduction to assessing the value of this variety of historical manuscripts.

BUSINESS, INDUSTRY, AND MANUFACTURING

Business, industry, and manufacturing includes producing goods or processing materials for commercial use, buying and/or selling goods for a profit, and lobbying for, assisting, or promoting business concerns. Important archives and manuscripts include those of single proprietorships, partnerships, corporations, or cooperative association; chambers of commerce, boards of trade, service associations, and benevolent associations; and individuals prominent in business, industry, and manufacturing activities.

Although there is an increasing amount of research about the nature of business records, there are still no studies that adequately describe the documentation of business, industry, and manufacturing; in fact, much that has been published in the business-oriented literature tends to discuss business and other organizational records as little more than interesting artifacts or public relations devices. The broadest description of business records is Francis X. Blouin, Jr., "An Agenda for the Appraisal of Business Records," in *Archival Choices: Managing the Historical Record in an Age of Abundance,* ed. Nancy E. Peace (Lexington, MA: D. C. Heath, 1984), pp. 61-80. Other good starting points for general information on business records are Edie Hedlin, *Business Archives: An Introduction* (Chicago: Society of American Archivists, 1978) and the special business archives issue of the *American Archivist* 45 (Summer 1982). An example of the new kind of studies being done on these records is JoAnne Yates, "Internal Communication Systems in American Business Structures: A Framework to Aid Appraisal," *American Archivist* 48 (Spring 1985): 121-40. There are also studies on specialized aspects of business record keeping, such as Dennis E. Meissner, "The Evaluation of Modern Business Accounting Records," *Midwestern Archivist* 5, no. 2 (1981): 75-100 and Richard W. Pollay, "Maintaining Archives for the History of Advertising," *Special Libraries* 69, no. 4: 145-54.

EDUCATION

Education includes all activities that encompass the education, training, and instruction of individuals. Important archives and manuscripts include those documenting public, private, and vocational education at the primary, secondary and post-secondary levels; individual school administrators, teachers, professional educators and educational theorists, and students; and groups formed to support, monitor, or change the educational systems.

Although there are numerous articles and other publications about college and university records, these generally concern their administration rather than appraisal or broader documentation; an example of this kind of publication is William Maher, *The Management of College and University Archives* (Metuchen, NJ: Scarecrow Press, 1992), although this author makes an effort to deal with the appraisal of such records and the documentation of such institutions. Frank Boles and Julia Marks Young, "Exploring the Black Box: The Appraisal of University Administrative Records," *American Archivist* 48 (Spring 1985): 121-40 is worth perusing, although this publication is more valuable for general appraisal practices than for understanding the role of the university in a locality or larger society. The most important starting place for archivists concerned with documenting education is Helen W. Samuels, *Varsity Letters: Documenting Modern Colleges and Universities* (Metuchen, NJ: Scarecrow Press, 1992), which is a model for determining first the salient functions of higher education which archivists should be concerned with documenting. Samuels has divided up higher education functions to be, as follows: confer credentials, convey knowledge, foster socialization, conduct research, sustain the institution, provide public service, and promote culture. She includes a model institutional documentation plan and a significant quantity of advice that every archivist should become familiar with in considering the appraisal/documentation of institutional records.

There is virtually nothing else written addressing the documentation of educational programs at any other level.

ENVIRONMENTAL AFFAIRS AND NATURAL RESOURCES

Environmental affairs and natural resources covers the utilization of natural resources (air, energy, plants, animals, minerals and water), their conservation and related environmental issues, and development of public policy concerning their use and conservation. Important archives and manuscripts include those of individuals involved in the use, conservation, and policy formulation regulating the use of natural resources; organizations established to promote the conservation, preservation, use and increased awareness of natural resources; and industries and businesses which make direct use of natural resources. A wide range of records are valuable for documenting this important topic, including personal and family papers, builders' and construction records for the built environment, probate records, legal records, government records, hospital and public health agencies, military medical records, and surveyors' records.

There are few descriptions of the documentation of environmental affairs and natural resources. One brief essay is David A. Clary, "The Archivist and the Human Environment," *Midwestern Archivist* 6 (no. 1, 1981): 35-45, but it is obvious that considerably more work is needed on this topic.

LABOR

Local documentation working groups need to examine how well organized labor is represented in historical records repositories. "Labor" is broadly defined as organized labor for the promotion of better working conditions, employment, security, and related concerns. Important archives and manuscripts include those of individuals involved with the development of organized labor; strikes, boycotts, or other labor-related events; and organizations such as labor unions and white collar employee associations. Also, archives and manuscripts that document working people and working conditions outside of organized labor should be well-represented in historical records repositories.

There is important work currently being done on labor documentation, although none has as yet been published. A general introduction to what has been going on in this area can be found in Philip P. Mason, "Labor Archives in the United States: Achievements and Prospects," *Labor History* 23 (1982): 489-97. Individuals involved in local documentation efforts will also note that there are specialized labor archives (such as at Wayne State and the University of Pittsburgh) and labor documentation experts who they can draw on for advice. Still, much of what has been written relates to the major labor unions, rather than all the facets of labor and its impact and importance in American society.

MEDICINE AND HEALTH CARE

Medicine and health care covers both pure and applied research in medical science and its service on the behalf of society through hospitals, clinics, and other health care organizations. Important archives and manuscripts that should be preserved include those of individual researchers, academics, and others prominent in medicine; individual physicians and health care personnel; corporations and businesses involved in applied research and delivery of services such as health care organizations and hospitals; government regulatory and funding agencies; and professional and other associations formed for the advancement, self-regulation, and promotion of medicine and health care.

Although some significant work in this topic is now going on, there is little published that local documentation working groups can effectively utilize; this will undoubtedly improve in the near future and individuals should watch for the appearance of new studies. A recent example of such work, and an important contribution to macroappraisal methodology, is Joan D. Krizack, "Hospital Documentation Planning: The Concept and the Context," *American Archivist* 56 (Winter 1993): 16-34 and her edited volume, *Documentation Planning for the U.S. Health Care System* (Baltimore, MD: Johns Hopkins University Press, 1994). Related studies that might be of some assistance are found under "Science and Technology."

MILITARY

Military is defined as the prosecution of war or insurrection, civilian participation in wartime activities, military installations and sites, peacetime military enterprise, and organizations formed to support military action, soldiers, and other related activities. Important archives and manuscripts include those of individuals who participated in the military or in support services to the military; civil defense, economic impact, and other aspects of civilian participation; installations and sites and other examples of the military presence in the state; and organized groups to support military action, soldiers, veterans, and other issues through lobbying, education, and promotion.

There are presently no quality studies that consider the broad documentation of military matters in society.

POLITICS, GOVERNMENT, AND LAW

Political, governmental, and judicial activity affects all inhabitants of a locality. Such activity creates and administers laws, provides many services, and protects the rights of citizens. Important archives and manuscripts for documenting this area include those of individuals active in political affairs, holding appointed and elected public positions, and involved in judicial activities; local and county government agencies and programs; state and federal agencies and programs with important ties to the locality and region; and organizations and movements seeking political change or encouraging participation in the political process.

No study has been done of the broad concerns in documenting politics, government, and law in society. Typical of the writings more descriptive in nature is H. G. Jones, *Local Government Records: An Introduction to Their Management, Preservation, and Use* (Nashville, TN: American Association for State and Local History, 1980). The pioneering appraisal writing for government archivists, with influence far beyond government and politics, is T. R. Schellenberg, "The Appraisal of Modern Public Records," *National Archives Bulletin*, no. 8 (Washington, DC: National Archives and Records Services, 1956). There are, however, some studies that examine specific aspects of this topic. Local repositories receive offers of the papers of state legislators or members of Congress; three studies that can guide decision making here are Paul I. Chestnut, "Appraising the Papers of State Legislators," *American Archivist* 48 (Spring 1985): 159-72; Patricia Aronsson, "Appraisal of Twentieth-Century Congressional Collections," in *Archival Choices: Managing the Historical Record in an Age of Abundance*, ed. Nancy E. Peace (Lexington, MA: D.C. Heath, 1984), pp. 81-104; and Lauren R. Brown, "Present at the Tenth Hour: Appraising and Accessioning the Papers of Congresswoman Marjorie S. Holt," *Rare*

Books & Manuscripts Librarianship (1988): 95-102. Another study that provides some insight in documenting specific political events and trends in localities is Don E. Carleton, "'McCarthyism Was More Than McCarthy': Documenting the Red Scare at the State and Local Level," *Midwestern Archivist* 12 (no.1, 1987): 13-19. Richard Brown, "Records Acquisition Strategy and Its Theoretical Foundation: The Case for a Concept of Archival Hermeneutics," *Archivaria* 33 (Winter 1991-92): 34-56 is an interesting introduction to the macroappraisal approach being developed by the National Archives of Canada. Related to Brown's essay and describing this Canadian repository's approach to modern case files is Terry Cook, " 'Many are called but few are chosen': Appraisal Guidelines for Sampling and Selecting Case Files," *Archivaria* 32 (Summer 1991): 25-50. The work coming out of the National Archives of Canada, typified by Brown and Cook's essays, is worth careful watching by individuals interested in the broader documentation approaches.

POPULATIONS

Populations encompasses a wide range of activity and groups including ethnic and racial groups; population movements of immigration, migration, and emigration; process of settlement; distinctive aspects of living in small communities or rural and urban areas; and special population groups such as children, elderly, disabled, and women. Important archives and manuscripts include those of individuals and families; ethnic and racial organizations formed to promote immigration or to assist immigrants and minorities; organizations formed to assist and lobby for special population elements such as the elderly and handicapped; and with unique value for documenting the experience of the various populations such as minorities, special social groups, and those living in distinct areas of the state such as small towns, rural settings, and urban environments.

Because of the tremendous interest in social history over the past two decades, a number of studies have appeared concerning the implications of such research on historical records repositories. Two general articles on this matter worth reading are Fredric M. Miller, "Social History and Archival Practice," *American Archivist* 44 (Spring 1981): 180-90 and Tom Nesmith, "Archives from the Bottom Up: Social History and Archival Scholarship," *Archivaria* 14 (Summer 1982): 5-26. Other useful publications on more specific aspects of this topic are Donald L. Fixico, "The Native American Researcher: Another View of Historical Documents," *Midwestern Archivist* 8, no. 2 (1983): 5-15; John A. Fleckner, *Native American Archives: An Introduction* (Chicago: Society of American Archivists, 1984); Janice Reiff, "Documenting the American Family," *Midwestern Archivist* 3, no. 1 (1978): 39-45; David E. Kyvig, "Family History: New Opportunities for Archivists," *American Archivist* 38 (October 1975): 509-19; Dale C. Mayer, "The New Social History: Implications for Archivists," *American Archivist* 48 (Fall 1985): 388-99; Eva S. Moseley, "Sources for the 'New Women's History,'" *American Archivist* 43 (Spring 1980): 180-90; Robert M. Warner and Francis X. Blouin, Jr., "Documenting the Great Migrations and a Century of Ethnicity in America," *American Archivist* 39 (July 1976): 469-77; and Rudolph J. Vecoli, "Diamonds in Your Own Backyard: Developing Documentation on European Immigrants to North America," *Ethnic Forum* 1 (September 1981).

RECREATION AND LEISURE

Recreation and leisure is defined as sports, hobbies, travel and group activities when leisure time is available. Archives and manuscripts essential for the documentation of this topic are those of individuals participating in administering or planning such activities; businesses directly associated with leisure activities such as resorts, health clubs, and professional sports teams; and cultural organizations such as literary societies and special interest clubs.

At present, there are no major analyses regarding the documentation of this topic. The article by T. D. Seymour Bassett, "Documenting Recreation and Tourism in New England," *American Archivist* 50 (Fall 1987): 550-69 is an encouraging example of the kinds of studies needed on this topic.

RELIGION

Religion is a topic that affects most of society and is defined as its role, organized and personal, for individuals, institutions, and society. Important archives and manuscripts include those of churches, synagogues, and religious denominations; organizations formed to promote religious activities such as lobby and special interest groups and independent camps and youth programs; individuals active in churches, denominations, and religious organizations; individuals whose papers reflect the significance of religion in everyday life; and specific activities, events, or religious movements important to the locality's history and development.

Three excellent essays that describe the unique aspects of religious records are Robert Shuster, "Documenting the Spirit," *American Archivist* 45 (Spring 1982): 135-41 and James O'Toole, "What's Different About Religious Archives?" *Midwestern Archivist* 8 (no. 2, 1983): 5-15 and "Things of the Spirit: Documenting Religion in New England," *American Archivist* 50 (Fall 1987): 500-17. Another publication useful for understanding church institutional archives is August Suelflow, *Religious Archives: An Introduction* (Chicago: Society of American Archivists, 1980). The best recent effort to develop a scheme for documenting an aspect of religion is *A Heritage at Risk: The Proceedings of the Evangelical Archives Conference July 13-15, 1988* (Wheaton, IL: Billy Graham Center, Wheaton College, 1988).

SCIENCE AND TECHNOLOGY

Science and technology encompasses both pure research and its applications to society for its benefits. Archives and manuscripts essential for documenting this topic include those of individual researchers, academics, and others prominent in scientific and technological fields; corporations and businesses involved in applied research and delivery of services such as manufacturers of information technology; government regulatory and funding agencies; and professional and other associations formed for the advancement and promotion of science and technology.

The topic of the documentation of science and technology has been well described because of the work of the Joint Committee on the Archives of Science and Technology (JCAST) and projects at individual archival institutions such as the Massachusetts Institute of Technology Archives and the American Institute of Physics. This work has been described in Clark A. Elliott, ed., *Understanding Progress as Process: Documentation of the History of Post-War Science and technology in the United States* ([Chicago]: JCAST, distributed by the Society of American Archivists, 1983) and Joan Krizack Haas, Helen Willa Samuels, and Barbara Trippel Simmons, *Appraising Records of Contemporary Science and Technology: A Guide* (Cambridge: Massachusetts Institute of Technology, distributed by the Society of American Archivists, 1985). For a description of the important work of discipline history centers, in this case the American Institute of Physics, refer to Larry J. Hackman and Joan Warnow-Blewett, "The Documentation Strategy Process: A Model and a Case Study," *American Archivist* 50 (Winter 1987): 12-47. For a proposed application of the documentation strategy model to science and technology, see Philip N. Alexander and Helen W. Samuels, "The Roots of 128: A Hypothetical Documentation Strategy," *American Archivist* 50 (Fall 1987): 518-31. A case study of documenting a complex corporation is Bruce H. Bruemmer and Sheldon Hochheiser, *The High-Technology Company: A Historical Research and Archival Guide* (Minneapolis: Charles Babbage Institute, Center for the History of Information Processing, University of Minnesota, 1989), a study which introduces the interesting concept of documentary probes. Finally, an excellent introduction to the documentation of modern science is Joan Warnow-Blewett, "Documenting Recent Science: Progress and Needs," *OSIRIS*, 2nd series, 7 (1992): 267-98, an essay which summarizes the most important work and describes remaining needs in the documentation of modern science.

SOCIAL ORGANIZATION AND ACTIVITY

Social organization and activity covers a broad range of human endeavor, including activities, lifestyles, problems, and the changing nature of ways of coping with life by individuals, families, and special groups. Important archives and manuscripts include those of individuals and families that reveal the nature of domestic and family life; organizations such as benevolent societies and auxiliaries formed to support their members or institutions; individuals involved in and groups formed to lobby for or promote special interests such as opposition to social injustice, reform, rights, and societal changes; associations formed to promote the interests and standards of occupations and professions; and philanthropic, charitable, and welfare agencies and associations formed to assist certain underprivileged or disadvantaged elements of society.

Most of the serious research in this topic has been done in social welfare, although such studies are valuable introductions to the challenges of documenting this area. These studies include R. Joseph Anderson, "Public Welfare Case Records: A Study of Archival Practices," *American Archivist* 43 (Spring 1980): 169-79; David Klaassen, "The Provenance of Social Work Case Records: Implications for Archival Appraisal and Access," *Provenance* 1 (Spring 1983): 5-26; and Klaassen, "Achieving Balanced Documentation: Social Services from a Consumer Perspective," *Midwestern Archivist* 11, no.2, (1986): 111-24.

TRANSPORTATION AND COMMUNICATIONS

This topic is defined as the development and impact of transportation and communications in the locality. Archives and manuscripts crucial to this topic's documentation include those of individuals prominent in the development of such systems or whose papers reflect the impact of these systems; businesses involved in the promotion, development, and offering of systems such as air, ground, and water transportation, newspapers, television and radio stations, and public relations and advertising firms; and government agencies and regulatory bodies with responsibility for transportation and communication services.

This is a topic that is only beginning to be examined thoroughly. Products of research such as Rosemary Bergeron, "The Selection of Television Productions for Archival Preservation," *Archivaria* 23 (Winter 1986/87): 41-53 are just beginning to appear.

NOTES

1. Edward F. Barrese, "Adequacy of Documentation in the Federal Government: Accountability Through the Record," *Information Management Review* 5 (Spring 1990): 54.

2. *The Control Revolution: Technological and Economic Origins of the Information Society* (Cambridge, MA: Harvard University Press, 1986), pp. 34-35.

3. For my further thoughts on the nature of cooperation, see *Strengthening New York's Historical Records Programs: A Self-Study Guide* (Albany: New York State Archives and Records Administration, 1988), section four, and *Managing Institutional Archives: Foundational Principles and Practices* (Greenwich, CT: Greenwood Press, 1992), chapter seven.

4. Once this selection is made, the proposed documentation strategy model can be followed. For more information on this see Section Three of this guide and Larry J. Hackman and Joan Warnow-Blewett, "The Documentation Strategy Process: A Model and a Case Study," *American Archivist* 50 (Winter 1987): 12-47.

5. By "representatives" I mean that not *every* institution, repository, or user group must be included in the process, otherwise the group would be too unwieldy in size. Individuals of the most important organizations and user groups, and the most knowledgeable about the locality's documentation and history, should be included. Especially in the initial stages, the composition of the advisory group will change as the best group is developed.

6. The objectives need not be considered final or precise at this early stage; they are to be used only to stimulate discussion and additional work.

7. The preliminary use of the documentation worksheets needs to be carefully explained. Their use is intended to facilitate initial discussion and not to be final, accurate evaluations. Such use of these worksheets should help the advisory group to identify areas of consensus and disagreement regarding the documentation of the locality.

8. The level of detail and time expended in this effort should be kept under control. It should be remembered that the idea here is to develop a general profile of the locality's documentation.

9. If a local repository with a quarterly journal or newsletter can be persuaded to publish progress reports, this publicity will be an excellent means to stimulate additional discussion and to maintain a focus on the documentation work.

10. The steps outlined in this phase generally follow the steps described in the Hackman and Warnow-Blewett essay, "The Documentation Strategy Process." (See note 4.) Refer to it for more information.

11. These actions include primarily the revision of acquisition policies, identification and preservation of key records, and establishment or enhancement of institutional archives.

12. See, for example, Judith E. Endelman, "Looking Backward to Plan for the Future: Collection Analysis for Manuscript Repositories," *American Archivist* 50 (Summer 1987): 340-55.

5

ARCHIVAL APPRAISAL AND THE EDUCATION OF THE ARCHIVIST: SOURCES AND COURSES

At the Spring 1992 meeting of the Midwest Archives Conference I served as a commentator on a session devoted to the "Documenting Milwaukee" project. Funded in 1989, the two-year project was intended to test the archival documentation strategy concept. Milwaukee had been selected because of the array of archival repositories in the urban region, interest in the project, and leadership from some knowledgeable archivists and prominent archival repositories.

My comments in this capacity had more to do with the importance of the Milwaukee effort than with the actual details of the project itself. I noted that we could debate the mechanisms and tools used in this effort, critique how they were applied in Milwaukee, analyze whether Milwaukee was the best site choice or not, and so forth. But I thought then that there was a far more important issue that should be moved to the forefront of the archival profession's discussion—the nature and purpose of archival appraisal. In this sense, I stated that what was being carried out in Milwaukee was not a luxurious, extracurricular effort by some of our colleagues made possible by the largesse of one of our federal granting agencies; what was being described was what should be the norm in archival appraisal, carried out through normal institutional resources. I came not to praise or to bury archival documentation strategies, but instead to tell archivists that they are essential to archival appraisal.

What archivists should focus on are basic definitions for appraisal that should be applied to the Milwaukee project as criteria for measuring its effectiveness or success. First, what is archival appraisal? It is the scientific identification of records possessing archival value and worth preserving in some form. Note, it is not primarily art or subjective process, but it is guided by specific principles and guided towards specific objectives. Those who adhere to art or subjectivity open the archival profession up to chaotic selection. There is documentation that is essential, and it is this essential documentation that we are after. And, what is more, every adequate appraisal process should lead archivists to the essential documentation time after time and that documentation should be generally the same unless it is guided by faulty appraisal. I noted, in those comments, that it should be obvious that the Milwaukee project suffered in this because it had to build on generations of faulty archival appraisal and, furthermore, the project had to try to rectify fuzzy thinking that has often plagued our work in appraisal and acquisition.

Second, what is the objective of archival appraisal? It is to document society and its institutions and organizations. It is not to collect materials for historians or other researchers, but it is to identify and preserve the transactional records that best document a specific activity or function, organization, event, or the like. It is first for the records creators and then to benefit others. It is focused on institutions or organizations because these produce transactional records and document our diverse populations. Again, the Milwaukee project only began to get at this essential purpose in its two-year effort because of a legacy of poor work which it had to overcome.

Third, what are the guiding values for archival appraisal? It is first, and foremost, evidential value. Evidential value is assigned to those records deemed by the creator to have permanent value for documenting activities and functions, protecting legal rights, and supporting ongoing administration. Informational value is not a guiding principle because it has never been adequately defined, and because it is often used in a sloppy manner to cover a multiplicity of poor appraisal decisions. I am not sure about the value of certain records so I state that the records have "informational" value. It also opens the door to archivists saving everything, for all records potentially have value to someone. Proper definition of documentary objectives for organizations and institutions and society leads us to evidential value. Informational value is a subset of evidential value; that is, the evidence of our organizations can benefit other researchers. The Milwaukee project never got to this point.

Fourth, who is responsible for the identification of archival records and for their maintenance? This identification is the responsibility of institutional records creators, not collecting historical manuscript repositories. The archival profession should primarily be in the business of fostering the development of institutional archives. Collecting programs should only be involved as repositories of last resort or to preserve the papers of important individuals not represented in institutional holdings. To collect otherwise is to border on unethical practice, because it removes the necessity of institutions maintaining their own records. The Milwaukee project was moving in this direction.

The only time we should diverge from the above definitions or guiding principles is when public interest demands us to do so, a point which Terry Cook has made well in his writings on archival appraisal. Particular public interest intercedes to tell us we should save certain records. Note, it is public interest and not arcane scholarly historians' interests. The same principle should be at work in our institutions when we find records important for use such as in current litigation and similar exceptional cases.

The archival documentation strategy as a mechanism helps us to determine first documentary goals and then to lead us to the records of evidential value. The documentation strategy guides us to the institutions which the archival profession should encourage to preserve archival records. It helps archivists to see how documentary goals cut across institutional records creators. The strategy helps us to determine how to use various methods and tools such as sampling and reappraisal. Because of its involvement with records users and custodians it also helps us to identify public interest.

The linchpin in the formation of obstacles to such basic archival principles for appraisal and acquisition is the poverty of our present educational programs. What do I mean by this, and what does this have to do with archival appraisal or the documenting of localities, the topic of this book? I am stretching for a very simple point. Our educational programs, both graduate and continuing, do not prepare archivists to know much about the principles and methods, let alone the theories, of archival appraisal. One bit of evidence for this is the experiences of projects such as conducted in Milwaukee, in which a common knowledge of appraisal objectives, theories, and practices was lacking, hindering an effort to develop more systematic approaches to documenting a locality and a region. Additional evidence is the problem encountered in a series of workshops (between 1987 and 1991) on the archival documentation strategy. We (myself, Tim Ericson, and Helen Samuels, who codesigned and cotaught this series) came to the conclusion that there was a compelling lack of knowledge about archival appraisal literature and approaches. The most important evidence is the lack of adequate education on appraisal being offered by the graduate archival education programs. In the 1993-94 Society of American Archivists Education Directory only one program (the University of Pittsburgh School of Library and Information Science) offers an identifiable full course on archival appraisal. This lack of educational programs creates a serious problem in which continuing education workshops, such as on the preparation of acquisition policies or archival documentation strategies, have little to start with except the apprenticeship form of training on the job, and there is little evidence of innovation, research, or experimentation here that would strengthen the archivist's depth of knowledge about archival appraisal.[1]

A COURSE IN ARCHIVAL APPRAISAL

In this concluding chapter I have included a summary of a course description for archival appraisal in a program in which I teach. I have included this summary for three reasons. First, it deals directly with the issue of the typical working archivist's lack of knowledge of archival appraisal theory, methodology, and practice. Second, and more importantly, it demonstrates the value of the archival documentation strategy concept as an organizing principle for educating an individual about archival appraisal. Third, it serves as an introduction for the description of the archival and related literature on archival appraisal and the documentation strategy approach.

Before describing this course, it is necessary to provide a little context for its place in the University of Pittsburgh graduate archival education program. The appraisal course is one of three advanced courses in the present archives curriculum. Students can take three introductory courses (Archives and Manuscripts Management, Records and Information Resources Management, and Library and Archives Preservation) which acclimate them to the archival field, its basic principles and practices, the nature and development of record keeping, and a variety of other similar matters. The appraisal course is offered as an opportunity to devote more specific attention to the basic archival functions (the archival students can also focus on archival arrangement, description, and reference and preservation management). After these courses, courses on specific applications of archival science, such as in local government or science and technology fields, are offered.

The appraisal course has two purposes. First, and most importantly, it provides a review of the basic theories, principles, techniques, and methods that archivists use for identifying and selecting (appraising) information with continuing or enduring value. The course is constructed on the assumption that appraisal is one of the most important responsibilities of the archivist and anyone intending to work as an archivist must be knowledgeable about this function. Second, the course provides an opportunity to compare and contrast archival appraisal to related activities in other fields, such as library collection management and development, artifact selection by museum curators, and the analysis of documentary evidence by historians. Again, another assumption is that archival appraisal, and the techniques and models that have developed to support this function, represents one of the unique contributions of the archivist to the information professions—the ability to determine what portion of information needs to be saved to document institutions, communities, society, and the people who make them up. Supporting both aims is a practical assignment in appraising an organization's records, forcing students to apply the principles which they have learned in the classroom to the practical challenges of appraising a set of records. Students satisfactorily completing this course have a thorough foundation for approaching the appraisal of records in their later work in archival positions.

The course is divided into five major sections. The first section is an introduction to the course, outlining what will occur during the term, what the learning objectives are, and the course requirements. The second section is a multiweek introduction to the definitions, theories, and principles that support archival appraisal. Students are introduced to the classic writings on appraisal theory and principles and the challenges of selecting records that possess continuing or enduring value. A portion of this section is devoted to reviewing some of the main debates about the purpose and practice of appraisal, especially the issue of the ideology of appraisal and the objectivity versus subjectivity of archival appraisal decisions.

Section three reviews prevalent appraisal practices and methods, from analysis of individual documents to institutional approaches to multi-institutional, cooperative appraisal efforts. In section four a series of case studies on archival appraisal are reviewed. These vary from year to year, depending on the nature of new work completed on archival appraisal. A typical approach would be to have two case studies focus on institutional appraisal (government and college and university), another on a topical area (science and technology), another on the geographic context of appraisal (documenting localities), and the remainder on the impact and challenges of recording media on archival appraisal (electronic, audiovisual, and visual records). The differences and similarities, strengths and weaknesses of these approaches are considered and contrasted. During the final section of the course students compare archival appraisal to similar functions in other disciplines.

Each student is expected to complete a lengthy set of readings and to participate regularly in class discussions. The course is conducted like a seminar, with class discussions based on the readings; each of the weeks' topics is supplemented by introductory lectures. A significant portion (one-third) of the student's grade is based on participation in class, and the instructor reserves the right to assign brief critical papers on the readings if class participation is insufficient. The remaining portion of the grade (two-thirds) is based on successful completion of an appraisal project at a local repository culminating in a detailed written appraisal report and the preparation of a major paper on some theoretical or practical application of archival appraisal.[2]

Each student is required to prepare a paper (20-25 pages) on some aspect of archival appraisal that interests them. The paper should be an in-depth review of a particular issue, technique or application, or principle that is essential to the archival appraisal function. Examples of acceptable subjects for this kind of paper include the matter of objectivity in the appraisal process, the appropriateness of sampling as an appraisal tool, and the importance of provenance to conducting archival appraisal. Students may also opt to write a comparative analysis of archival appraisal with some other library or information science function. Examples of acceptable subjects for this kind of paper include a comparison of archival appraisal criteria to library preservation selection criteria and the archival concept of intrinsic value as compared to evaluation criteria used by material culture experts. This paper is worth one third of the course grade.

While there is a considerable number of readings, the articles and books provide only a introduction to the complexities and challenges of conducting archival appraisal. The literature also introduces the student to the debates within the archival community about how appraisal should be carried out. Overall, the aim is to have the student learn to think like an archivist in the realm of appraisal and acquisition and, upon completing the course, to possess a problem-solving perspective on conducting such work in a specific institutional environment.

As mentioned, the course commences with a focus on appraisal definitions, theories, and principles. Students learn where appraisal fits into the broader archival administration as practiced in particular places. What is appraisal? How has it changed over the past twenty-five to fifty years? What are the major differences between the 1977 and 1992 Society of American Archivists (SAA) basic manuals on this topic?[3] What are some of the major debates, in North America, about the role, scope, and objectives of archival appraisal? All of these questions can be considered through a growing quantity of readings.[4] The two SAA manuals on appraisal provide a contrast to the changing nature of archival appraisal—Brichford emphasizing records characteristics and the quality of use as an indicator of successful appraisal and Ham stressing models and processes such as the acquisition policy and broader conceptual models meant to define basic appraisal objectives.

These questions, and efforts to formulate tentative answers, lead to a consideration of what I call the "traditional foundations" of archival appraisal theory and practice, as reflected in the writings of pioneer European and North American archivists such as the Dutch Muller, Feith, and Fruin, the English archivist Jenkinson, and Schellenberg and Margaret Cross Norton in the United States.[5] These latter writings introduce archival students to the basic thinking about appraisal from the 1890s through the 1950s, leading to the classic formulations of values such as evidential and information. These formulations continue to be the takeoff point for appraisal discussions and debates even in the 1990s.

Considering these earlier writings help archival students to realize several characteristics of their professional literature. First, they realize that the issue of appraisal has been the topic of long-term debate and concern. Jenkinson's argument for archival selection to be made by the records creator rather than the archivist always prompts lengthy and soul-searching discussion by the students concerning the larger mission and objectives of archival appraisal. Second, the students also realize that some of the more recent debates are not new in topic, tone, or substance; Norton's writings, as just one example, appear strangely modern despite being written in the 1920s through the 1940s. Finally, the archival students are reintroduced to the relationship of some of the basic archival principles to appraisal, such as the orderly organic nature of records emphasized by the Dutch archivists in their landmark 1898 manual of archival practice. A related benefit is the increasing number of essays which can provide an international perspective on the development of archival appraisal thinking and practice.[6]

A contrast to the early formation of archival appraisal concepts is the early introduction of archival students to the problem of historical knowledge and documenting the past. While there is a voluminous literature addressing this matter, I have found that David Lowenthal's *The Past Is A Foreign Country*[7] is an excellent introductory tool for students to gain some understanding of this particular challenge. Lowenthal addresses the matter of how our sense of the past is determined, and he includes lengthy descriptions of the role of documents and written documentation in this process. There are other brief essays that provide stimulating incentives for considering similar issues. Daniel Boorstin has penned an elegant essay about the matter of the survival of documentation and the impact on its interpretation, and Kenneth Foote has provided an intriguing contribution on archives as a part of society's "memory conservation."[8]

A fundamental aspect of understanding archival appraisal is to realize its ideological implications. In the past archivists have primarily couched this discussion in the context of objectivity versus subjectivity in conducting appraisal. But there is considerably more to this than that contrast, a debate that has permeated most professions and disciplines in their research. Here American archival students have had access to some of the writings of European archivists, most notably Hans Booms. This German archivist has written within the parameters of a debate between East and West which focused on the East's subservience to a Marxist-Leninist ideology in performing appraisal.[9] Despite the fact that Booms' target is a more dramatic one, his writings still aid the students in realizing the potential dimensions of larger ideological frameworks which might govern or affect ultimate appraisal decisions. His writings also lead to a questioning of the degree of difference between Jenkinson's assertion that the records creators make at least the first selections and the more rigid political orientation of the former Eastern Bloc countries; might not the end results be possibly the same?

There are other writings that enable the archival student to consider the ideological aspects of making appraisal decisions. Some are extremely forthright in their assessment that archivists need to be sensitive to underrepresented groups, often the more powerless sectors of our society.[10] Others have concentrated less on this matter, but they have stressed that even the most basic definitions of archival terms and functions shift in meaning and use through the years.[11] These kinds of explorations, and more are definitely needed, suggest that students need to consider carefully the meaning of such basic words in the earlier published discourses by archivists on every topic, including appraisal. The essays on the matter of reappraisal relate directly to the changing notion of what goes into the archives and, as well, the reliability of previous appraisal decisions and how previous appraisal work should be viewed by contemporary archivists.[12]

After an introduction to the basic nature and purpose of archival appraisal, and some of the stickier aspects represented by the ideological dimensions and historical knowledge, students then devote a number of weeks to a full consideration of archival appraisal methods and practices. The structure for this part of the course—item and collection approaches, collection policies and institutional archives, and cooperative and multi-institutional methods—developed from my participation in the documentation strategy seminars. In those seminars we determined that, in addition to describing the nature and process of the strategy, we needed to relate it to other archival appraisal methodologies and tools. It was obvious to us that the documentation strategy filled in some gaps in archival appraisal theory and practice and, as well, helped to determine when to use certain appraisal tools and approaches. In the appraisal course students learn about the item level approaches such as intrinsic value,[13] sampling,[14] and more proactive efforts such as working within the offices of elected officials to assist in the identification of archival records.[15] All of these approaches are only most useful when viewed in the light of larger documentary objectives and the basic values usually associated with appraisal work. Some of the writings on collection level appraisal issues also relate to the knowledge of particular subject fields associated with the records fonds; while there are few exemplary studies in this regard, there are some that dramatically reveal why it is important for archivists to understand a function, activity, event, or discipline.[16]

Students are then introduced to the concept of acquisition policies and other appraisal approaches employed by archival programs. Models of appraisal decision making provide students with a sense of both how appraisal ideally might be conducted and as a benchmark for determining how it is actually working.[17] The archival acquisition or collecting policy is very useful for discussing the purposes of archival appraisal (because such policies require a description of what the repository wants to acquire or document) and for beginning to build bridges between institutional appraisal priorities and the multi-institutional approaches such as the documentation strategy. In this area, some very useful and thought-provoking literature has been published, ranging from a framework for developing such policies,[18] to evaluating their effectiveness,[19] to relating the creation and use of such policies to broader documentary goals.[20] Equally impressive has been the recent discourses on using management, communications, and other theories and models as a template for evaluating the appraisal of institutional archives.[21] These articles help the student consider both the unique aspects of appraising such records and how the appraisal process relates to that used by collecting repositories.

The next segment of class discussion is cooperative and multi-institutional appraisal methods and practices, a session which focuses more directly on the archival documentation strategy. The kinds of readings used are described later in this chapter, but they include the familiar writings of Helen Samuels, Larry Hackman and Joan Warnow-Blewett, and Terry Cook. This class discussion is the concluding segment in the section on archival appraisal methods and tools, and it leads to appraisal case studies that provide students with the opportunity to look at a topical or geographical area or institutional type to see how appraisal has been conducted, refined, or criticized. Because students also have a practical assignment to prepare an appraisal report, this part of the course becomes the most relevant for their learning. Fortunately, an extremely interesting and useful body of case study literature has developed in the past decade.

The initial case study area is in science and technology, chosen because of its pioneering role in archival appraisal and the strong literature (theoretical and practical) to support it. Science and technology also comes first because it was in this environment that the conceptual aspects of the documentary strategy were formed and tested. The logical point of departure is the report of the Joint Committee on Archives of Science and Technology, which provides a detailed and interesting account of the records of these disciplines and recommendations for their thorough documentation.[22] A volume that needs to be read in close conjunction with the JCAST study is the appraisal manual prepared by a group of archivists of MIT. This study is the first serious analysis of the nature of documentation of any particular disciplinary area.[23] It first seeks to understand the various functions and activities of science and technology, then considers the resulting kinds of records and information generated by them, and finally examines various approaches for adequately documenting the functions and activities.

The third major volume in science and technology is the study of one high technology company, introducing a different means of appraising records via "documentary probes." These probes are used to gather up all the necessary documentation of certain organizational activities and functions when these activities and functions have been identified as crucial to understanding the institution.[24] Other interesting essays by nonarchivists also relate to appraisal and documentary concerns, including one recent, if inconclusive, article on the documenting of a recent scientific controversy which was aired out more in the electronic pathways than by way of print and more traditional forms of records.[25]

Another fruitful area for documentation and appraisal study is that of government. Government documentation is especially important since much of the original concepts of appraisal emerged from the work and thinking of government archivists in North America and abroad; Jenkinson, Schellenberg, and Posner are just a few of the names that come to mind in this regard. Interesting new approaches and challenges to traditional methods continue to emerge from the government sector, both providing excellent case studies for the use of students. One major overview of government records programs was completed because of the concern that electronic information technology was outstripping the normal means of archivists to ensure that essential archival records were being maintained.[26] Archival students can also examine fairly traditional policies and methods, such as those associated with joint archives-records management programs, for guidance in the appraisal of the mountain of government records.[27]

It should not be surprising that students can also be introduced to archival appraisal approaches which have failed. The National Archives' experimentation with the notion of "adequacy of documentation" was the result of the separation of records management from this archival institution in 1985 and also an interesting concept which the National Archives backed away from despite intense interest by the larger archival profession about its viability.[28] The failure of the appraisal of the Federal Bureau of Investigation records is a case study in the limitations of standard records management scheduling.[29] Moreover, a latter article describing the nature of, and resources for, appraisal at the National Archives is additional testimony as to why such standard approaches have been less than successful.[30] The avoidance of examining government published documents is another problem, one which has not been satisfactorily addressed by the archival profession and which shows how its approach to the universe of records and information sources has been somewhat hamstrung.[31] Still, students need to understand that despite such limitations intriguing new appraisal concepts are still emerging from government archives, not unlike the period of the 1930s and 1940s —the heyday of Schellenberg and Jenkinson.[32]

There are other institutional types which can be used as case studies for studying appraisal. In these other areas the writings are less systematic and not as useful for didactic purposes in an archives course. As indicated, a great portion of archival institutions and historical manuscript repositories have a local focus, but the topic of thorough documentation of localities has not been a major one in the archives literature. In this regard, studies in historical method, ethnography, and anthropology reveal some interesting problems for how and why individuals collect materials with some relationship to documenting localities.[33] Even more useful are the divergence of writings on colleges and universities. The archival community now possesses a very standard, traditional manual on the administration of college and university archives[34] and a ground-breaking study on the functional, macroappraisal approach to the documenting of colleges and universities.[35] These two volumes provide an excellent contrast for archival students to understand more typical and newly developing approaches to the documentation of such major institutions as those of higher education.

The appraisal course concludes with one class session devoted to an examination of the implications of special media for archival appraisal and another session that considers related work in other disciplines. This is, unfortunately, a stop-gap measure in lieu of having a full course to deal with the challenges posed by electronic media and other records such as photographs and visual materials. Electronic records have generated the greatest quantity of writings, although they display an extremely wide range of opinions about their relationship to archival functions such as appraisal. Most of the early writings on the appraisal of electronic records focused on large statistical data bases, and in this area the articles and reports are clear, concise, and concrete for the students.[36] More recent writings have described newer approaches stressing political, policy, and technological solutions, all of which stimulate discussion concerning the different means of successfully appraising archival records.[37]

The studies on other media, such as photographs and motion pictures, are extremely important to introduce students to the limitations of current archival appraisal methods and principles. How, for example, does a framework of evidential and informational values hold up against the visual nature of such records? How does even the standard definition of a document relate to a motion picture? When appraisal is considered, how is it conducted in the broader documentary context of photographs or motion pictures? Although these kinds of questions are only partially answered by the available publications, even the partial posing of such issues is useful for teaching appraisal.[38]

The course is completed with a brief session comparing archival appraisal approaches to those in other fields. Library science collection development/management writings have been very influential on the refinement of the archival documentation strategy, and it is also an excellent point to foster some conversation since many graduate programs are located in library and information science schools.[39] The challenge that history museum curators have faced in documenting or interpreting the twentieth century is not unlike that faced by archivists in conducting appraisal, and some of the essays on this topic make for some interesting comparisons as well.[40] Fortunately, there are also a few essays which attempt to relate material culture studies to the broader issues of documentation, including that represented by archives and manuscripts.[41]

In teaching appraisal, the archival documentation strategy has been extremely useful in two very basic ways. On the one hand, the documentation strategy, because of its multi-institutional, macroappraisal approach provides a structure for the basic course in archival appraisal. On the other hand, the archival documentation strategy helps the student to understand better the gaps in documentation and various appraisal techniques. The strategy's macroappraisal emphasis on what is to be documented draws attention away from detailed analysis of records to the broader purposes of appraisal and the archival profession. Not all is resolved, of course, but the student departs with a fuller understanding of the current strengths and weaknesses of modern archival appraisal.

WRITINGS ON THE ARCHIVAL DOCUMENTATION STRATEGY

Through the past decade a number of writings have appeared that define, refine, and contest the archival documentation strategy. These writings are described here to assist the individual to gain additional information about the concept of the archival documentation strategy.

The pioneer defining essay on the archival documentation strategy is Helen W. Samuels, "Who Controls the Past," *American Archivist* 49 (Spring 1986): 109-24. Samuels' essay portrays the documentation strategy as a concept and method which enables archivists to contend with the rapidly changing nature of modern documentation. Her essay, which mostly focuses on the nature of contemporary records, is a contribution to the theoretical foundations of archival appraisal. A more process-oriented introduction to the archival documentation strategy is Larry J. Hackman and Joan Warnow-Blewett, "The Documentation Strategy Process: A Model and A Case Study," *American Archivist* 50 (Winter 1987): 12-47. This essay describes how the strategy can be accomplished and contains a case study of the American Institute of Physics efforts over the years to document American and international physics. The best manner to approach an orientation to the documentation strategy is to read in tandem the Samuels and the Hackman/Warnow-Blewett essays. There are more recent efforts to describe the impact of the documentation strategy on archival appraisal theory and practice, including most notably Helen W. Samuels, "Improving Our Disposition: Documentation Strategy," *Archivaria* 33 (Winter 1991-92): 125-40, and Terry Cook, "Documentation Strategy," *Archivaria* 34 (Summer 1992): 181-91.

There are earlier essays which portend the mid-1980s birth of the archival documentation strategy. F. Gerald Ham's essays have proved to be seminal in the reanalysis of archival appraisal that led to the formulation of the archival documentation strategy as a concept and method: "The Archival Edge," *American Archivist* 38 (January 1975): 5-13; "Archival Strategies for the Post-Custodial Era," *American Archivist* 44 (Summer 1981): 207-16; and "Archival Choices: Managing the Historical Record in an Age of Abundance," in *Archival Choices: Managing the Historical Record in an Age of Abundance,* ed. Nancy E. Peace (Lexington, MA: D.C. Heath, 1984), pp. 11-22. These essays are among the most important and most oft-quoted of the appraisal writings. Andrea Hinding, "Toward Documentation: New Collecting Strategies in the 1980s," in *Options for the 80s: Proceedings of the Second National Conference of the Association of College and Research Libraries,* eds. Michael D Kathman and Virgil F. Massman (Greenwich, CT: JAI Press, 1981), pp. 531-38 is an earlier use of the notion of the documentation strategy but it overemphasizes collecting at the expense of other archival appraisal principles and methods. Other different kinds of cooperative efforts can be seen in the earlier development of regional and statewide collecting repositories, mostly located in the Midwestern states. James E. Fogerty, "Manuscript Collecting in Archival Networks," *Midwestern Archivist* 6, no. 2 (1982): 130-41 is a good example of the kinds of thinking that supported this variety of work, and the remainder of essays in that particular issue on networks can provide an excellent background for understanding their origins and evolution to that point.

The general placement of the archival documentation strategy in its broader framework of appraisal and acquisition was attempted by Richard J. Cox and Helen W. Samuels, "The Archivists' First Responsibility: A Research Agenda for the Identification and Retention of Records of Enduring Value," *American Archivist* 51 (Winter/Spring 1988): 28-42, one of three major papers trying to expand on the SAA's 1986 planning document. Other essays have also attempted to do the same, including Margaret Hedstrom, "New Appraisal Techniques: The Effect of Theory on Practice," *Provenance* 7 (Fall 1989): 1-21 who argues for the value of the archival documentation strategy as a viable new approach for dealing with the increasing challenges of modern documentation.

Although the critics of the documentation strategy argue that it has been untested, there are important exceptions to this which reveal the viability of this appraisal approach. Philip Alexander and Helen W. Samuels, "The Roots of 128: A Hypothetical Documentation Strategy," *American Archivist* 50 (Fall 1987): 518-31 is the best known and perhaps most appropriate of the assertions of use of the documentation strategy.

The discussion since the mid-1980s of the archival documentation strategy has also prompted considerable discussion about appraisal in general and the specific merits of the more strategic approaches. Frank Boles has been the most critical about the archival documentation strategy, arguing in his "Mix Two Parts Interest to One Part Information and Appraise Until Done: Understanding Contemporary Record Selection Processes," *American Archivist* 50 (Summer 1987): 356-68, that appraisal can only be successfully conducted from the particular priorities of institutions rather than multi-institutional cooperative approaches such as the archival documentation strategy. Terry Abraham, "Collection Policy or Documentation Strategy: Theory and Practice," *American Archivist* 54 (Winter 1991): 44-52 argues that the concept adds theoretically to the appraisal process but that it is untested, castigating the concept as the Holy Grail— illusionary—for archival appraisal efforts.

The nature of the criticisms directed to the archival documentation strategy has been around for a period of time considerably predating the introduction of the concept. Max J. Evans, "The Visible Hand: Creating a Practical Mechanism for Cooperative Appraisal," *Midwestern Archivist* 11, no. 1 (1986): 7-13 is an argument that while appraisal decisions should be shared, nevertheless, such appraisal work must be conducted fully within the context of individual institutions. Evans argues that there are no common standards in appraisal work, an argument worth further exploration and certainly one that reflects serious obstacles to multi-institutional or macroappraisal approaches such as the documentation strategy.

On the other hand for every essay such as Evans there is another which suggests reasons why the archival documentation strategy approach is needed in the archival discipline. David J. Klaassen, "The Archival Intersection: Cooperation Between Collecting Repositories and Nonprofit Organizations," *Midwestern Archivist* 15, no. 1 (1990): 25-38 is a well-reasoned and important argument for cooperation in aiding the protection of institutional archives, stressing the need to find a critical mass of resources and support in such cooperation. Klaassen's essay is an excellent counterpoint to the heavy emphasis in the North American archival profession on collecting. What his essay misses is an adequate treatment of how such nonprofit organizations can be identified as being worthy of the profession's attention. The documentation strategy approach can provide both a mechanism and criteria for identifying the important, unique, and essential organizations that should be thoroughly documented. The most important recent essay that places the documentation strategy in its larger archival theory context is Terry Cook's "Mind Over Matter: Towards a New Theory of Archival Appraisal," in Barbara Craig, ed., *The Archival Imagination: Essays in Honour of Hugh A. Taylor* (Ottawa: Association of Canadian Archivists, 1992), pp. 38-70. As Cook argues in this essay, the aspect of "what" should be documented takes precedence over other appraisal approaches and "appraisal is a work of careful analysis and of archival scholarship, not a mere procedure." The macroappraisal approach reflected in the documentation strategy concept certainly falls within such views.

It is likely that as the 1990s progress, there will be additional writings on macroappraisal approaches, such as the Samuels' functional analysis of colleges and universities, which demonstrates the validity and value of such appraisal theory and practice. Joan D. Krizack, "Hospital Documentation Planning: The Concept and the Context," *American Archivist* 56 (Winter 1993): 16-34 is an example of the new archival appraisal work being done on major aspects of our society.

NOTES

1. Archivists must realize that such innovation is needed to cope with the changing nature of the organizations they serve and document. See, for example, David Bearman and Margaret Hedstrom, "Reinventing Archives for Electronic Records: Alternative Service Delivery Options," in *Electronic Records Management Program Strategies,* ed. Margaret Hedstrom (Pittsburgh, PA: Archives and Museum Informatics, 1993), pp. 82-98.

2. This has been changed recently to a different assignment. Now students are required to prepare a report that evaluates the acquisition or appraisal policy of an archives, historical manuscripts, or records/information resources management program. These reports are intended to include a description of the policy, an evaluation based on related archival and records management standards, proposals for strengthening the policy and its use, and ways that the "success" of the policy could be measured.

3. Fortunately, we now have two basic writings far enough apart in time to reflect shifting emphases in the North American archival profession's thinking about appraisal. See Maynard J. Brichford, *Archives & Manuscripts: Appraisal & Accessioning* (Chicago: Society of American Archivists, 1977) and F. Gerald Ham, *Selecting and Appraising Archives and Manuscripts* (Chicago: Society of American Archivists, 1992).

4. A good starting point for a history of archival appraisal thinking is Nancy E. Peace, "Deciding What to Save: Fifty Years of Theory and Practice," in *Archival Choices: Managing the Historical Record in an Age of Abundance,* ed. Nancy E. Peace (Lexington, MA: D.C. Heath, 1984), pp. 1-18.

5. S. Muller, J. A. Feith, and R. Fruin. *Manual for the Arrangement and Description of Archives* (New York: H. W. Wilson, 1968), chapter one; Sir Hilary Jenkinson, *A Manual of Archive Administration,* rev. 2nd ed. (London: Percy Lund, Humphries & Co., 1966), pp. 136-55; T. R. Schellenberg, "The Appraisal of Modern Public Records," *National Archives Bulletin* 8 (Washington, DC: National Archives and Records Service, 1956); and Thornton W. Mitchell, ed., *Norton on Archives: The Writings of Margaret Cross Norton on*

Archival & Records Management (Carbondale: Southern Illinois University Press, 1975), pp. 231-65.

6. For example, Ole Kolsrud, "The Evolution of Basic Appraisal Principles—Some Comparative Observations," *American Archivist* 55 (Winter 1992): 26-39.

7. David Lowenthal. *The Past is a Foreign Country* (Cambridge: Cambridge University Press, 1985).

8. Daniel Boorstin, "A Wrestler with the Angel," in *Hidden History* (New York, 1988), pp. 3-23, and Kenneth E. Foote, "To Remember and Forget: Archives, Memory, and Culture," *American Archivist* 53 (Summer 1990): 378-92.

9. Hans Booms, "Society and the Formation of a Documentary Heritage," *Archivaria* 24 (Summer 1987): 69-107, and "Uberlie-ferungsbildung: Keeping Archives as a Social and Political Activity," *Archivaria* 33 (Winter 1991-92): 25-33.

10. Danielle Laberge, "Information, Knowledge, and Rights: The Preservation of Archives as a Political and Social Issue," *Archivaria* 25 (Winter 1987-88): 44-49.

11. James M. O'Toole, "On the Idea of Permanence," *American Archivist* 52 (Winter 1989): 10-25.

12. Leonard Rapport, "No Grandfather Clause: Reappraising Accessioned Records," *American Archivist* 44 (Spring 1981): 143-50; Karen Benedict, "Invitation to a Bonfire: Reappraisal and Deaccessioning of Records as Collection Management Tools in an Archives—A Reply to Leonard Rapport," *American Archivist* 47 (Winter 1984): 43-49; and Lawrence Dowler, "Deaccessioning Collections: A New Perspective on a Continuing Controversy," in *Archival Choices: Managing the Historical Record in an Age of Abundance,* ed. Nancy E. Peace (Lexington, MA: D.C. Heath, 1984), pp. 117-32.

13. *Intrinsic Value in Archival Material,* NARS Staff Information Paper 21 (Washington, DC: National Archives and Records Service, 1982).

14. Frank Boles, "Sampling in Archives," *American Archivist* 44 (Spring 1981): 125-30; Margery N. Sly, "Sampling in an Archival Framework: Mathoms and Manuscripts," *Provenance* 5 (Spring 1987): 55-75; Terry Cook, " 'Many are called but few are chosen': Appraisal Guidelines for Sampling and Selecting Case Files," *Archivaria* 32 (Summer 1991): 25-50.

15. Lauren R. Brown, "Present at the Tenth Hour: Appraising and Accessioning the Papers of Congresswoman Marjorie S. Holt," *Rare Books & Manuscripts Librarianship* (1988): 95-102; Patricia Aronsson, "Appraisal of Twentieth-Century Congressional Collections," in *Archival Choices: Managing the Historical Record in an Age*

of Abundance, ed. Nancy E. Peace (Lexington, MA: D.C. Heath, 1984), pp. 81-104.

16. David Klaassen, "The Provenance of Social Work Case Records: Implications for Archival Appraisal and Access," *Provenance* 1 (Spring 1983): 5-26.

17. For this Frank Boles and Julia Marks Young, "Exploring the Black Box: The Appraisal of University Administrative Records," *American Archivist* 48 (Spring 1985): 121-40 is extremely useful for didactic purposes. A research analysis of the effectiveness of this model is Frank Boles, *Archival Appraisal* (New York: Neal-Schuman, 1991).

18. Faye Phillips, "Developing Collecting Policies for Manuscript Collections," *American Archivist* 47 (Winter 1984): 30-42.

19. Judith E. Endelman, "Looking Backward to Plan for the Future: Collection Analysis for Manuscript Repositories," *American Archivist* 50 (Summer 1987): 340-55.

20. Timothy L. Ericson, "At the 'rim of creative dissatisfaction': Archivists and Acquisition Development," *Archivaria* 33 (Winter 1991-92): 66-77.

21. Michael Lutzker, "Max Weber and the Analysis of Modern Bureaucratic Organizations: Notes Toward a Theory of Appraisal," *American Archivist* 45 (Spring 1982): 119-30; JoAnne Yates, "Internal Communication Systems in American Business Structures: A Framework to Aid Appraisal," *American Archivist* 48 (Spring 1985): 141-48; and Francis X. Blouin, "A New Perspective on the Appraisal of Business Records: A Review," *American Archivist* 42 (Fall 1979): 312-20.

22. Clark A. Elliott, ed., *Understanding Progress as Process: Documentation of the History of Post-War Science and Technology in the United States; Final Report of the Joint Committee on Archives of Science and Technology* (Chicago: Distributed by the Society of American Archivists, 1983).

23. Joan K. Haas, Helen W. Samuels, and Barbara T. Simmons, *Appraising the Records of Modern Science and Technology: A Guide* (Cambridge: Massachusetts Institute of Technology Press, 1985).

24. Bruce H. Bruemmer and Sheldon Hochheiser, *The High-Technology Company: A Historical Research and Archival Guide* (Minneapolis, MN: Charles Babbage Institute, Center for the History of Information Processing, University of Minnesota, 1989).

25. Bruce V. Lewenstein, "Preserving Data About the Knowledge Creation Process: Developing an Archive on the Cold Fusion Controversy," *Knowledge: Creation, Diffusion, Utilization* 13 (September 1991): 79-86.

26. Victoria Irons Walch, "Government Records Programs: An Overview," in *Committee on the Records of Government: Report* (Washington, DC, March 1985), pp. 69-95.

27. David Levine, "The Appraisal Policy of the Ohio State Archives," *American Archivist* 47 (Summer 1984): 291-93, and Karen Paul, *Records Management Handbook for United States Senate Committees* (Washington, DC: Senate Historical Office, 1988) are examples which can be used.

28. Edward F. Barrese, "Adequacy of Documentation in the Federal Government," *Information Management Review* 5 (Spring 1990): 53-58.

29. Susan D. Steinwall, "Appraisal and the FBI Files Case: For Whom Do Archivists Retain Records?" *American Archivist* 49 (Winter 1986): 52-63.

30. Elizabeth Lockwood, "'Imponderable Matters:' The Influence of New Trends in History on Appraisal at the National Archives," *American Archivist* 53 (Summer 1990): 394-405.

31. Richard J. Cox, "Government Publications as Archives: A Case for Cooperation Between Archivists and Librarians," *Journal of Library Administration* 7 (Summer/Fall 1986): 111-28.

32. National Archives and Records Administration, *The Inter-Governmental Records Project: Phase 1 Report* (Washington, DC: NARA, July 1990) and Richard Brown, "Records Acquisition Strategy and Its Theoretical Foundation: The Case for a Concept of Archival Hermeneutics," *Archivaria* 33 (Winter 1991-92): 34-56 are examples.

33. Such as David E. Kyvig and Myron A. Marty, *Nearby History: Exploring the Past Around You* (Nashville, TN: American Association for State and Local History, 1982); John D. Dorst, *The Written Suburb: An American Site, An Ethnographic Dilemma* (Philadelphia: University of Pennsylvania Press, 1989), chapters 1 and 5; and Kevin Lynch, *What Time Is This Place?* (Cambridge: Massachusetts Institute of Technology Press, 1972), chapters 2-4.

34. William Maher, *The Management of College and University Archives* (Metuchen, NJ: Scarecrow Press, 1992).

35. Helen W. Samuels, *Varsity Letters: Documenting Modern Colleges and Universities* (Metuchen, NJ: Scarecrow Press, 1992).

36. Charles Dollar, "Appraising Machine-Readable Records," *American Archivist* 41 (October 1978): 423-30; Ross J. Cameron, "Appraisal Strategies for Machine-Readable Case Files," *Provenance* 1 (Spring 1983): 49-55; Harold Naugler, *The Archival Appraisal of Machine-Readable Records: A RAMP Study With Guidelines* (Paris: UNESCO, 1984).   For a full bibliography of writings on this topic see my "Readings in Archives and Electronic Records: Annotated Bibliography and Analysis of the Literature,"

in *Electronic Records Management Program Strategies,* ed. Margaret Hedstrom (Pittsburgh, PA: Archives and Museum Informatics, 1993), pp. 99-156.

37. Margaret Hedstrom and Alan Kowlowitz, "Meeting the Challenges of Machine-Readable Records: A State Archives Perspective," *Reference Services Review* 16, nos. 1-2 (1988): 31-40; John Mallinson, "Preserving Machine-Readable Records for the Millenia," *Archivaria* 22 (Summer 1986): 147-55; Alan Kowlowitz, *Archival Appraisal of Online Information Systems,* Part 2 of *Archives and Museum Informatics* 2 (Fall 1988); Advisory Committee for the Co-ordination of Information Systems. *Management of Electronic Records: Issues and Guidelines* (New York: United Nations, 1990); Michael E. Holland, "Adding Electronic Records to the Archival Menagerie: Appraisal Concerns and Cautions," *Provenance* 8 (Spring 1990): 27-44.

38. Sam Kula, *The Archival Appraisal of Moving Images: A RAMP Study with Guidelines* (Paris: UNESCO, 1983); W. H. Leary, *The Archival Appraisal of Photographs: A RAMP Study with Guidelines* (Paris: UNESCO, 1985); Cilla Ballard and Rodney Teakle, "Seizing the Light: The Appraisal of Photographs," *Archives and Manuscripts* 19 (May 1991): 43-49; Rosemary Bergeron, "The Selection of Television Productions for Archival Preservation," *Archivaria* 23 (Winter 1986-87): 41-53.

39. An excellent essay for this purpose is Ross W. Atkinson, "Selection for Preservation: A Materialistic Approach," *Library Resources & Technical Services* 30 (October/December 1986): 341-53. Also commentary by Margaret Child, pp. 354-62.

40. Harry Rubenstein, "Collecting for Tomorrow: Sweden's Contemporary Documentation Program," *Museum News* 63 (August 1985): 55-60, and Thomas J. Schlereth, "Contemporary Collecting for Future Recollecting," *Museum Studies Journal* 113 (Spring 1984): 23-30.

41. Nancy Carlson Shrock, "Images of New England: Documenting the Built Environment," *American Archivist* 50 (Fall 1987): 474-98.

Appendix A

Worksheet for Local Documentation Analysis

WORKSHEET FOR LOCAL DOCUMENTATION ANALYSIS

Topic	Definition/Comments	Rating/Evaluation of Documentation		
		Pre-1900	20th Century	Present

INDEX

Abraham, Terry, 166

Accounting, 135-36

Acland, Glenda, 36

Acquisition, vii; policy for, 52-55, 59, 62n46, 66, 79, 102, 113, 116, 120, 121, 158, 159

Adams, Herbert Baxter, 8, 12

Advertising, 2, 136, 145

Agriculture, 133-34

Alabama, 39, 40

Albada, Joan Van, 36

Alexander, Edward, 43-44

Alexander, Philip, 90-91, 144, 166

Amateur history, 12; in urban areas, 72. See also Antiquarians

American Archival Analysis, vi

American Association for State and Local History, xii

American Institute of Physics, 70, 144, 164

Anderson, R. Joseph, 145

Anthropology: and appraisal, 87-88

Antiquarians, 11, 12, 16-17, 18, 53; in urban areas, 72

Appraisal: and adequate documentation, 65-66, 112-13, 161; and archival education, 153-68; and chronological time frames, 56; and documentary gaps, 57-58, 79, 119-33; and historical manuscripts tradition, 35-37; importance, v, vi, 66-69, 149-51; and objectivity, 40-41, 47, 154, 157-58; problems, 42-51; and researchers, 68-69, 81-82, 83-84, 87-88; as a salvage approach, 104; theory, 46, 59-60. *See also* Acquisition; Collecting; Documentation strategy; Functional analysis; Macro-appraisal; Reappraisal; Record values; Sampling

Archaeology: collections, 77, 84

Archdiocese of Chicago, 92-93

Architecture, 21, 37-38, 134-35

Archives, 8; and the definition of locality, 9-11; and historical research, 11-13, 18-21; and the locality, 21-27; as a profession, 23, 83-84; theory, 23, 50. *See also* specific types of archives

Archives of Industrial Society, 74

Archives of Scientific Philosophy in the Twentieth Century, 74-75

Arronson, Patricia, xi, 140

Artifacts. *See* Material culture

Arts, 134-35

Association of Canadian Archivists, xii, 50

Audiovisual records, 155

About the Author

Richard J. Cox (A.B., Towson State College; MA, University of Maryland; Ph.D., University of Pittsburgh) is an Associate Professor in Archival Studies at the University of Pittsburgh, School of Information Sciences, where he is responsible for the archives concentration in the MLS degree. Prior to his current position he worked at the New York State Archives and Records Administration, the Alabama Department of Archives and History, the City of Baltimore, and the Maryland Historical Society. Through the years Dr. Cox has been very active in professional archival associations, especially the Society of American Archivists (SAA), for which he was a member of the society's governing council from 1986 through 1989 and served as editor of its journal, the *American Archivist,* from 1991 through 1995. He has written extensively on archival and records management professional issues with numerous articles. He was also principal author of a major evaluation of Alabama's historical records, *Assessing Alabama's Archives* (1985) and a self-study guide for New York's historical records programs, *Strengthening New York's Historical Records Programs* (1988), winner of the Arline Custer Memorial Award given by the Mid-Atlantic Region Archives Conference for publishing excellence in the field of archival administration. Dr. Cox also won the Custer Award in 1979. He is the author of *American Archival Analysis: The Recent Development of the Archival Profession in the United States* (1990), on the development of archival professionalism in the United States in the 1980s; this book won the Waldo Gifford Leland Award, given by the Society of American Archivists. More recently, Greenwood Press published his *Managing Institutional Archives: Foundational Principles and Practices* (1992) and Haworth Press his *The First Generation of Electronic Records Archivists in the United States: A Study in Professionalism* (1994). Dr. Cox was named a Fellow of the Society of the American Archivists, that association's highest honor, in 1989.

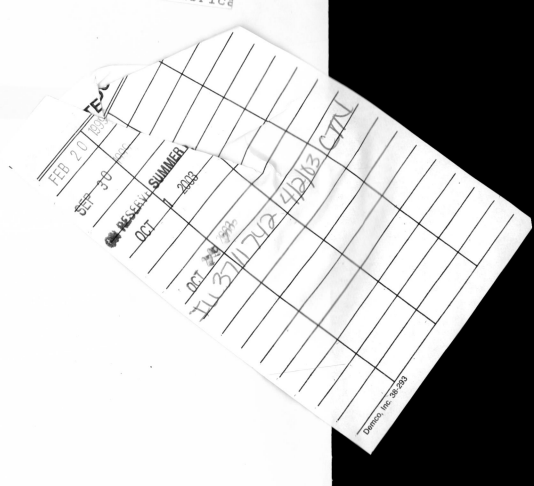